# WHY YOU'RE STILL SINGLE OR IN A SHITTY RELATIONSHIP

Frank Di Genova

Allow Right Now Publishing

Toronto. Canada

Frank Di Genova/Allow Right Now Publishing
Toronto, Canada
www.frankdigenova.com

Book cover design, editing and formatting by Frank Di Genova

Why You're Still Single Or In A Shitty Relationship/Frank Di Genova — 1st ed.
ISBN Paperback 978-0-9951596-7-9  ISBN eBook 978-0-9951596-8-6

POLARIZED
RELATIONSHIPS

*Dedication*


Dedicated to everyone who desires a loving and passionate relationship.

To every woman who broke my heart and played with my head. You were my greatest teachers.

# Contents

# WELCOME & DISCLAIMER

Welcome to *Why You're Still Single, Or In A Shitty Relationship*. Thank you for choosing this book and for investing in yourself. The universe has mysterious ways of bringing together those who share their knowledge with those who seek it. Your desire and my teachings have crossed paths. "Ask and it will be given to you; seek and you will find." When you're ready to open the door, it will open. Or you may not be ready and we've collided simply by chance. Regardless, my offering will either plant a seed for later when you're more receptive or totally piss you off.

In any case, if this material doesn't resonate with you, reject it. When we hear something new that challenges our current belief system, we can experience abreaction. If you do, I invite you to look at what you're resisting. Typically we're not triggered by anything unless it aggravates an unhealed wound. Why else would you defend it? You can bypass the pain, or you can face it and begin to heal.

The content in this book is by no way going against anyone's freedom of expression, beliefs, choice of sexual orientation or gender identity. No one should deny anyone's motive or equality for their choices. I'm inclusive and an ally of the LGBTQ2S+ community.

Having said this, my views expressed here are from a heterosexual standpoint. I can't speak for anyone who identifies with a different sexual orientation or expression than my own. Doing so would be ignorant and bigoted. If pronouns are important to you, I'll be using *he/she, him and her.* This content deals with the masculine and feminine energy between monogamous cisgender males and females. Nonetheless, what I'm sharing can be profound and bring a deeper understanding of the masculine and feminine energy embodied in whatever gender you choose to identify as.

These writings are my opinions and observations from my personal life experiences. They're also from research on varying spiritual, biological and scientific conclusions. I can only write about what I know empirically and what I've experienced personally. Nevertheless, some topics are explored and shared based on highly probable albeit theoretical concepts. I declare my right and freedom to express myself as I choose.

My writing style may appear harsh and bold; I also use generalizations to convey typical gender tendencies. Obviously, not all men or women are cut from the same cloth, as there are many exceptions. I'm clarifying now to avoid having to add disclaimers before *each* questionable example. Although the subject matter is significant, my approach is good-natured banter. You will notice grammatically, the way I write uses contractions; get used to it. Although I'm not responsible for your reactions, it's not my intent to disrespect or offend you in any way.

# WHO AM I TO SAY?

Who am I or what authority do I have in writing this book? After thirty-six years behind the hairstyling chair; many failed attempts at finding happiness through dating and relationships, and a thirst for wanting to know why; I can confidently say I'm qualified to tell you *what not to do*. Although I've learned a lot, no one is ever truly done unless they choose to stop. I'm always looking to gain more clarity and wisdom. Looking back, I could have blamed everyone except myself for all the failures I've experienced. It would have been much easier but would've kept me stuck. I chose instead to take responsibility and cut through all the layers of my ignorance, assumptions, anger and confusion. I needed to know why I had a hard time sustaining any kind of meaningful relationship.

I wrote about relationships in my previous books, with the understanding I had then. As I climbed the spiral staircase of experience, I learned and integrated more wisdom; thus affording me a better vantage point. You'll notice this evolution by leafing through my past work. You'll find the material there quite beneficial. For most, what I've shared is enough. Yet, something vital was still missing, I didn't know what it was, but *I felt it.* The answer kept eluding me and I sensed it was close; it was like a lost key sitting at the bottom of a pond. I knew it was just a matter of finding it and pulling it out. The question was, "How?" I needed something to draw it toward me. Little did

I know the secret could be found in the very thing that could retrieve the key. The power of a magnet; it's the foundation of this book. You'll understand this more as you read through and integrate the teachings I will be sharing.

I've spent many hours mulling over if I should share my personal story. Since doing so in great detail throughout my first book I didn't think it was necessary reiterating. A part of me felt it was important, but the other thought it would be redundant. Then there's the imposition of having read it. Since you're here now, it only makes sense to carry it out. A backstory is important, and for you to trust anything I say, I need to come clean and share my experiences *authentically*. I decided to make a compromise, to truncate my previous offering and add newer and more relevant events. What follows is an *objective* approach; reconciling the majority of my past has allowed me this perspective. There are always more layers to uncover and heal, the journey never ends. This isn't a sob story, nor am I vying for your pity. It's simply *feedback* from what I've learned during my experiences.

My past has helped me get to where I am now, and I trust its wisdom will help you navigate through your travels with more ease. What doesn't kill you does make you stronger, but it also teaches many unhealthy coping mechanisms. Some of which almost killed me. I've landed on my feet and have become stronger because of it. Another reason I didn't want to share my struggles is, generally, women don't want to hear a guy spew his emotions all over the place. If this sounds sexist, then keep reading.

I can remember the exact day when the light went on in my head and when I had the *breakthrough*. It happened while dating a younger and very masculinized woman. By this I mean her behaviour, not physically because she was beautiful. I don't know if I just had enough of being ignorant or if she was the catalyst I needed. She did what my mother, former wife, and every relationship with dominant women couldn't do. Once I had the *ah-ha* moment, it all made sense, as if the stars suddenly aligned. Magically, the universe began confirming this realization by showing me constant signs. The muddied window became clearer. Before I share this with you, I invite you to take a trip with me down memory lane.

My mother and twin brother abandoned me during a tragic and premature birth experience. My brother was stillborn and drowned from the fluid in his amniotic sac; which forced me out sooner than planned. My mom technically died, she had flatlined until receiving five blood transfusions. I did reunite with her after spending a month in an incubator. Finally, after almost thirty days apart, I felt her touch and heartbeat. As a result, I missed out on the boob thing and was robbed of forming a bond with her. I've heard the lack of somatic touch can cause babies to die, even if they were well-fed. Yikes, luckily, I had the nurses there to change my soiled diapers. As a result, I suffered from separation anxiety, and for most of my life, I lived in fear and panic. I was super sensitive, hyper and developed trust issues. I stuttered and never felt safe, connected, comfortable or grounded in my body. The awareness of others watching me walk would cause me to stumble and trip over myself. I felt naked, on display, and self-conscious. It wasn't until my eighth year when learning about my brother that I suffered from survivor's guilt.

My parents were loving people, Italian and all about protecting the family. They did the best they could to help me along. Perhaps to compensate and show gratitude for their miracle baby, they spoiled me rotten and gave me everything, except for what I needed. They didn't have the awareness or emotional capacity to satiate my extraordinary needs; it was like asking a fish to climb a tree. I was constantly wanting to feel safe and validated. The die had been cast and the remedy I sought from them transferred to everyone I met thereafter. I was smothered and coddled with love, food and material things, but it wasn't what I needed. Unbeknownst to them, I was parched emotionally and not dying from thirst.

Being resourceful, I learned how to cope and organically my persona took shape. Although I was mischievous and a little devil, I had a heart of gold and deeply cared for people. I was super empathic and felt everything, but I had to bury it all inside, nobody understood me. I also had charisma, it was powerful and I could sweet-talk my way out of just about anything. It was my safeguard and the only tool I had. I was the star of my show, an untouchable.

When I was eleven, my sister was born—*then bam*—she got all the *attention*. Suddenly, from owning the centre stage, I exited stage left. Although I loved her deeply, it was hard on me. The smoke screen and the safety my theatrics provided quickly dissipated, my armour and shield had been torn away; stripped naked. Instead of fighting for attention, I reverted to a passive and introverted baby. The kid who never grew up; the boy who suffered from Peter Pan Syndrome.

During my early life, I've endured a few traumatic events, some had been violent and others sexual. These experiences closed me off even more, I felt betrayed and my trust was broken further. My teenage years had been spent filled with anger and feeling wronged by everybody; and with life in general. This time coping wasn't performed by a boy wearing a green tunic and tights. In its place was an epic performance, camouflaging pain, anger, confusion, and fear via alcohol and other bypassing behaviours. My shield was humour, also being the class clown and playing the cool guy. I became a desperate emotional pauper seeking acceptance as an acquiescent *yes-man*. I lacked confidence and was quite impressionable. I was betraying my very being, selling out and hating myself for it. All I wanted was to be *heard* and *understood*, to *feel safe*, for someone to *get me*, and to understand what I *needed*. I thought having a good woman would make my life complete. I worked hard and followed the cultural narrative which had been set before me.

Fast forward, by the age of twenty-seven, I had it all. I was married, devoted, had a child and a car paid off. My mortgage was low enough that I could begin to relax and enjoy life. But I was so stressed you couldn't ram a pin up my ass with a jackhammer. I did all the right things, but it was never enough. I never felt valued or appreciated, no matter how hard I tried. No matter how much I did for my wife or others, I felt taken advantage of. The disillusionment sunk me to new lows and it was devastating. I turned to God for answers, to save me, not for my soul, but from destroying myself. I was in a very dark place, full of anger and betrayal; I was suicidal. I meditated two hours a day, fasted for days and became a vegetarian. Nothing helped me. What else did I have to do to prove my worth? The squeaky wheel always gets oiled right? No... I felt like even God bailed on me.

No one could play the victim any better than I did. I sought refuge in another serious relationship, but it only magnified the wounds I was avoiding. In desperation, I learned the love languages and raised the bar even higher in my service to my then-partner. It only left me feeling exploited and unappreciated yet again. As you may surmise, I'm not a fan of that love language book. I was riddled with guilt and questioned if I'd made a mistake getting divorced. Could it get any worse?

In just six months, I lost my young mother to cancer and a thriving forty-one-year family-owned business, which was due to a condo development. Adding that, I had previously lost two domestic homes and an investment property. My health was declining, I was overweight and drinking excessively. Financially, emotionally and physically, I was a mess. I always found a way to bypass responsibility for my ill decisions. *Frank was the greatest victim alive.* I realized during my life I used it to manipulate others, especially women. Somewhere along the way, I learned how to activate women's maternal and nurturing instincts. I got them to feel sorry for me. It was done unconsciously, and of course, I thought it was just my good looks and charming ways. I did have the Kavorka though, Seinfeld fans will know this term (The lure of the animal). I had the power to seduce women very easily.

There was a problem, I was too nice. Sure, I'd get them, but just as fast, they'd run off into the arms of some asshole. I both despised and admired these selfish pricks who women seemed to gravitate uncontrollably toward. I envied their magnetic ability to lure them in but hated how they always ended up hurting them. Why wasn't being a good and caring guy enough? Not for my mother, former wife, ex-common law, and now this young masculine woman. The more I did for them, the more I felt rejected. My self-worth dropped to *zero*. Naturally, I ended up angry at all women.

Being out of options, I decided to learn the art of pick-up. I got really good at it too, I not only impressed myself but also my friends. The hotter the women were, the easier it was to seduce them. Now for the caveat; the once Mr. Nice guy became a very toxic and self-loathing asshole. Sure I was attracting hotties, but it was all surface, void of depth and connection. I became the jerk I hated. Looking back, I realized I was seeking revenge on every woman who'd ever hurt me. The art of pickup isn't what I'll be teaching here. Men do not become healthy or masculine by learning *picku*p because it's pure manipulation.

In a vibrational world, like attracts like, I was wounded and so were the women I had attracted. Secretly I tried to fix them, which would confuse them even more. Why? Because I only wanted a FWB; but oddly, I would do committed relationship types of things. Like being romantic, treating them like queens, kissing them on their forehead and encouraging them to fall for me. I gave them mixed messages (how could I not?) I was inconsistent with myself, a dichotomy. Deep down, all I wanted was another's approval and to be loved—someone to get me, and to be *enough*. How is this possible with a closed heart, being emotionally unavailable and afraid to get hurt again? Deep down I cared for these women while trying to convince myself I didn't. My life was a lie, I had nothing to show for all my pain and suffering. Sadly, I believed *suffering and pity was the only way to earn love and acceptance.*

I found spirituality in my mid to late teens and I thought it was the answer to everything ailing me—it was the ticket out of my miserable existence, an attempt to make sense of my life. I've since learned, spirituality is only part of the picture and is not the full painting. The guilt of being a jerk haunted me, so I got to work on healing that. I learned everything I could and was initiated into many healing modalities. I practiced ancient pranayama and meditation techniques and did some crazy cosmic shit. I was no longer aspiring to be the *elusive cool guy*, I became the spiritual dude. I believed the spiritual path was the way I'd meet my life partner, twin flame, soul mate, or whatever the term of the week was. She'd be the one who understood me and help make all my pain go away. I became a Sensitive New Age Guy (SNAG).

Little did I know being a SNAG added to the problem and it was pushing every potential woman, even further away from me. I also stopped believing in *Twin Flames*. Almost all my partners thought I was *The One*. My feelings for them weren't the same, so how could this be true? We are only supposed to have one twin flame right?

I couldn't understand what was wrong. To further rub salt in my wounds, I was the quintessential renaissance man. Who can resist a guy who's spiritual, good with his hands, can do any home renovation, loves to cook, cleans toilets, does energy healing, writes music, sings and plays guitar, gives killer massages, and can be their personal-hairstylist? I've been told I'm also a great kisser and a great catch. *So why the hell why was I still single?*

Well, I was a bit needy, craved attention and was still too nice. My hairstyling job did entail pleasing women and catering to their needs, so I was still approval-seeking. Could it have been the 2 AM drunk texts and not respecting boundaries? Was it because I still had wounds and trauma to address? Did my financial situation have anything to do with it? Was it because I put too much pressure on women... and myself? I was always questioning, "Is she *The One*, or maybe it's her? No, it's this one, but she doesn't check off every box on my list. What's her sign? Damn, it's not compatible with mine. No, I can't date an Aries. Is she holistic and spiritual? Does she understand EMFs and toxins in our food, air and water? Nope, her smartphone runs on a different operating system. It'll never work." I'm embarrassed to say how bad it truly got. She had to be perfect. Surprisingly, these weren't the reasons why I was single. Even if every box was checked, it wouldn't make any difference.

As a young man, I had been drawn to cute tomboys. Then as a teenager, I was pulled toward the girly girls in high heels, long painted nails, red lipstick, lingerie, and so on. Then something happened when I got into the spiritual world. Suddenly, for some reason, those overly feminine women used to repulse me. They were too delicate, dainty, overly emotional damsels in distress. I perceived them as being materialistic, shallow and opportunistic. Ironically, at the same time, I was fascinated with strippers, hookers and porn stars. Still, semi-dormant was my desire for lipstick, lingerie and the sultry femme fatale. I didn't want to sleep with them, I was attracted to the power they possessed to seduce without getting caught up in feelings. I always wanted them to like and validate me. Are you noticing a pattern? There was something deeper at play here, and I couldn't see it... even if I did.

Sexually insatiable women drove me crazy. They possessed something I desired, but I didn't know what. I equated their energy with the power of a Goddess. As a result, I began seeking spiritual chicks. Not the flaky and erratic ones who talk to crystals and sage their food, but the self-sufficient, non-material, down to Earth ones. If they had short nails, no polish or makeup, hair in a ponytail, a T-shirt and jeans—I was cooked. In short, I wanted a shaman hippy who shaved her legs and armpits—tomboy meets scandalous sexy hybrid. To land her, I signed up for yoga, went to trade shows and spiritual expos, and later became an exhibitor myself, to sell my books. I put myself out there in the hopes of finding her. I found many mermaids who were actually sirens in disguise. They captivated me with their beauty and song; only to leave me emotionally shipwrecked against the rocks of despair.

I attended countless spiritual meetups, retreats and workshops. This rocker party animal needed to upgrade his energy if he was to meet his Goddess, right? I was always the only guy in these groups. The women there were many years older, or much younger than me. They were jaded, angry, hating men and the world, or naive and just getting their feet wet. The younglings were often confused and trying to understand where they fit in. They were still looking for their purpose and what they wanted in life. Was I stuck in the middle, born ten years too soon, or too late? Maybe it was another excuse or ignorance toward what was truly happening? The irony was, I believed through spirituality, I was finding myself, but it was the exact opposite. My balls were turning into ovaries, and my penis was shrinking into a clitoris. I was lost and engulfed in feminine energy; believing it was enlightenment. The truth was, I was bypassing yet again, this time escaping into the unseen.

The hope of finding my person was fading fast. I wasn't going to meet my soul mate in a bar or nightclub, let alone in the spiritual community. Dating apps were a joke and seemed like a waste of time. In truth, I wasn't going to meet her anywhere; if I did, I'd probably fuck it up anyway. That's what almost happened with this younger and masculinized woman. Even though it didn't work out between us, she gave me the greatest gift of all... *the secret to why I was perpetually single and in shitty relationships for most of my life.* I finally figured out why there wasn't any chemistry between us. She was as spiritual as I could ask for, younger, highly educated, accomplished, natural, and unmotivated by material things. It seemed like the perfect fit.

I learned why I was repeatedly triggered and defensive around her. Why I was anxious and needed to always prove myself. What was I angry at? I feel guilty on some level because she was the catalyst I needed to finally understand; *learning at her expense.* I have deep compassion for her and for all the trauma she had to endure in her life. She mirrored virtually everything I'm sharing in this book. Nonetheless, I was ready, and the Universe responded. I believe it always answers us in some way. It was obvious, I wasn't ready to listen before.

Years back at a party, a woman told me something I didn't fully grasp then. She advised me to hold my cards closer, and not to share everything so soon. "Keep the mystery up Frank, you are sharing too much and getting deep too fast. Save it for when someone gets to know you better." Maybe I was trying to prove myself and in doing so, scared women away. Wasn't sharing vulnerabilities and feelings, laying it all on the line, talking about spirituality and opening my heart what women wanted? No, it's far from it. This woman planted yet another seed which would sprout almost a decade later.

Everything I've learned until this point in my life prepared me for my awakening. All it took was one domino to fall to collapse the entire narrative. Everything started to make sense and it couldn't be changed. Like beliefs, they're only mental constructs propped up by what we think and want to be the truth whether they're false or not. The truth was, I attracted masculine women because they had what I needed to embody within myself. I mistook their dominance for having confidence; *things I lacked*. I wasn't standing in my power and was forfeiting my role as a man. I didn't know it then, but I was emasculated, needy and craved approval. I finally discovered what *masculine* and *feminine* polarity truly was, and how it's the catalyst for every healthy relationship. I found the *magnet* and the answer I was looking for.

# CHAPTER ONE

# RELATIONSHIPS TWIN FLAMES & ORGASMS

## WHAT IS LOVE?

I'm quite tempted to type Haddaway's song lyrics of begging my baby not to hurt me anymore. I think the mischievous little cherub called Cupid causes more pain when he decides to impale someone with those poison-dipped arrows of his. Some call it a pesky love potion and others say it's hormones. According to a team of scientists led by Dr. Helen Fisher at Rutgers School Of Arts and Sciences, they conclude, romantic love can be broken down into three categories: *lust, attraction* and *attachment*. Each class can be characterized by its own set of hormones. Testosterone plus estrogen creates *lust*—dopamine, norepinephrine and serotonin produce *attraction*, and oxytocin plus vasopressin forms *attachment*. Are we simply causalities of these cocktails, or is there more to it?

Have you ever truly loved someone unconditionally? Or was it just a transactional occurrence? Looking back, I don't know if I've truly known what real love was. Sure, I loved my parents and son, but beyond that, it was probably just different forms of lust and dependency. There was always a motive; I wanted someone to *complete me,* or at least help ease my burden. If I couldn't love myself then maybe someone else could take on that responsibility. Maybe, they could be able to appreciate the parts of me I couldn't. Why do we seek love?

True love just *is,* it is *innate,* all-inclusive and independent. Conditional love needs to be earned and sought out. When we find it, we cling to the fear of losing it. I believe *true love* is something which cannot be defined by words. Many people mistake love to be an emotion, but it's not. It's a state of being; independent of all conditions. What does love mean to you?

Whether you're looking for a soulmate, twin flame, life partner, fuck buddy, or your person, it's usually to fulfill a need. The motive may not always be apparent. There's a saying, "We meet someone for a *reason,* a *season* or a *lifetime."* The real *reason* is to *season* us so we can be with our *lifetime.* Along the way, we meet many soul mates who help us *innerstand* and recognize our *completeness,* by showing us our incompleteness.

At our core we are whole and unaccompanied, every relationship offers an opportunity to become conscious of this. We learn from each other, each lesson is not exclusive. A relationship offers mutual growth and healing, but most see it differently. We try to fix and conform our partners to what we *need* them to be. We become defensive and blame them for not *complying,* or failing to *complete* us. We fail to understand we're with them because they're showing us what we need to learn about ourselves. We will bargain, threaten, and try manipulating them into catering to our needs. The relationship becomes *conditional* by the demands we impose on them; so they can prove our lovability and validate their love for us. *"If you loved me, you'd do this, or you wouldn't do that."* Those who do comply may also suffer similar insecurities and need for approval.

We may feel they aren't doing enough, which causes us to believe they don't care. We compare our efforts with theirs or overcompensate to please them, and this puts an unfair burden on them. We then get angry when we feel they're not reciprocating. Eventually, this leads to resentment and the breakdown of the relationship. Why do we believe our partners are mind readers and should *just know* what we need? We all have different ways to show and communicate love. What we think we want isn't always what is best for us, we don't really know. When we have an expectation, disappointment follows. Our higher self knows exactly what we need; so surrender and be open to whatever presents itself.

## RELATIONSHIPS

A relationship can be with a parent, child, friend, family member, *yourself* and certainly a lover. If you break down the word relationship, you get *re-lat-ion* and *ship*. Re means *back* or *backward* and also stands for again. *Lat* signifies to *carry, ion* means to *go*, and *ship* is *quality* or *condition*. A ship also means a vessel, something you are on. *Re-lat* means brought back, or bring something—in the relation to something else; recounting of a connection. How are you relating with another, or even yourself?

Imagine sitting in a chair alone in a dark room. You can't see or hear anything, it's only you and your thoughts. Now ask, "Who Am I?" You may know the answer immediately, or you may be more confused than before I asked. I'm not going to get too deep here because you can read my other books for that. Just for a moment bear with me. In this room, you're a cipher, a non-entity without anything to compare yourself to. All your knowledge and memories lay dormant until they're activated. Someone else needs to animate them and bring them to light. This defines who you are, but who are you? Are you your thoughts, beliefs or emotions? Are you what you've been told, or what you should be?

We wear many costumes and associate with several identities. We can be all of them, yet at our core, we're none of them. Every morning when we arise we put on a new mask, or a different face. Is it the same one day after day, week after week, or year after year? *Which character* or personality is your go-to? I'm not talking about wearing makeup or a costume for Halloween. Speaking of *witch character*, psychologists say the costumes we choose are an attempt to explore and express hidden aspects of ourselves without inhibition. Ladies, so what's with the witch and slutty police outfits all about? Costumes not only reflect how we want to appear to the world, but they're also a protection which hides those parts we're afraid to show and express. We also use masks as a distraction and to fit in. So what am I getting at here?

Without knowing who you are, you may modify yourself to match better with your partner, so they accept you. Maybe you expect them to alter themselves for you too? This is how we lose ourselves.

Dream analysts say every character in your dreams represents different parts of you. Spiritual gurus often say everyone in this dream (waking life) is also an extension of you and mirrors back hidden parts of yourself that you can't or don't want to see on your own. These reflections are both *desirable* and *undesirable*. What you admire or hate in another reflects how you feel about those traits within yourself. If someone triggers you, they're stirring up hidden wounds for you to discover and heal. We're also projecting our shadow outward for others to see and process. You can decide to look deep into your reflection or break the looking glass. This isn't an easy process, as it's hard to face undesirable traits in ourselves. Meet yourself impartially through every interaction you have with others. Relating to others is how we grow and evolve.

Notice how differently you act with everyone you know. Have you ever tried rekindling a past relationship and realized all the same shit comes up? This also happens when we meet old friends by chance, or at school reunions. Sometimes the dynamics are the same, or they're much different. People change, or they don't. There may come a time when you'll grow apart from someone and can no longer relate to them. You've evolved, or they have. Their reflections are no longer relevant to your growth. Alternatively, not being triggered by another affords you the ability to meet them on their level without judgement (which is self-judgement). This allows you the opportunity to enjoy their company authentically... or not.

You can choose to be single where no one challenges you, or you can go on a self-exploring adventure with others. You may believe going solo is the easier way, but even if you choose solitude, you're still entangled with your *thoughts, beliefs* and *emotions.* Our memories are indicators and understandings of where we've been and they also give us context to know what to work on. You may try hiding them from others and yourself, but sooner or later, they'll surface. There are merits to doing inner work and also having others help draw out your shadow.

## WEDDING VOWELS

Did you know that married men live longer than single men? It's true, but they are more willing to die.

"I take you to be my wife/husband, to have and to hold from this day forward, for better or for worse, for richer or for poorer, in sickness and in health, to love and to cherish, to unconditionally love and accept your meddling mother, your over-talkative father, alcoholic brother, creepy uncle, bitchy sister, your freeloader friend who always causes a scene, your ex-wife/husband, and step kids from this day forward until death do us part."

On a serious note, be mindful when getting involved with another. You're committing not only to one person but to a *minimum of six people.* Not just *u* and *i*, but the *a, e, o's* and all the *consonants.* You're getting the whole package, and then some. You marry all their parental patterning, varying ethnicity, cultures; religious and belief systems, and all related causes and effects. You also wed all their emotional and sexual hang-ups, guilt, shame, insecurities and possible traumas. You'll also have to deal with each of their past relationships or lovers who may have jaded them. They say you're the product of the *five people* you hang out with most, but your partner can make or break you. They will affect your mental and emotional health, life choices and finances. Just like one rotting fruit in the basket can ruin all the rest.

In the past, only for a short time, I treated women badly. The reason was due to the pain inflicted on me *by those who I thought loved me.* I bled on women who didn't cut me but did on those who picked at the scabs. Only *hurt people hurt people;* you may be the *victim* or the *assailant.* You can perpetuate these patterns by taking the easy path and blame others, or you can grow up and take responsibility. We attract what we *need,* not what we *want.* Do you want to be on a *relation-ship* or a *battle-ship?* Having a healthy relationship is dependent on your internal state of being. If you aren't right inside, a relationship won't make it better, it'll make it worse. The things you seek will amplify the issues you're trying to avoid. Ironic, isn't it?

If you don't heal before entering a new relationship, you'll re-traumatize yourself and possibly your partner. Not addressing your past, its traumas, and your inability to communicate will bring you more of the same. If you feel a relationship is the end game and will make you happy, you're mistaken. Seeking another to solve your problems is *codependence* and *toxic.* Likewise, the information in this book is not an instant fix. If you're not ready to do the work, you're wasting your time. You'll be on an endless spin cycle and repeat the same patterns until there's no one left to blame. One day you may snap out of it when you're tired of sitting on the couch eating ice cream *(cry scream)* or drowning your sorrows in a bottle. These only give temporary relief, as do orgasms.

## SEXUAL ENERGY IS THE CREATIVE FORCE

Everything we do sexually is the desire to feel the creative force. Spiritually speaking, from our birth we've been disconnected from this Divine Source (Unconditional love). We mistakenly attempt to reclaim it by seeking it externally, resulting in temporary fulfillment and conditional love. We often seek another's affection in the hope it fulfills us. Unless you spend hours, days or years meditating in a cave, an orgasm is the closest you can get to God. We know this inherently, and desire to feel it again. In its absoluteness, sexual energy is Divine Energy. When we realize this, sex can become our path to Samadhi, or enlightenment. Unfortunately, we view sex and orgasm as an end and not a means to it. The Sacred union becomes selfish and carnal, then it's just fucking.

We often mistake *happiness* and *pleasure* as being the same thing, as we do between *sex* and *intimacy*. Although appearing similar, they're different. Pleasure releases dopamine which can become addictive and result in withdrawal symptoms. Feeling happy coincides with naturally occurring serotonin levels, which doesn't lead to compulsive behaviour. Like dopamine, an orgasm can become addicting; like drugs, it'll never be enough. Choose your delivery system, a crack pipe, a rolled-up bill, or your genitals, it's all the same. It's like eating a bag of potato chips because no matter how many orgasms you have, you always want more to sustain the high. Our logical brain (the critical thinking part) shuts down and goes on vacation during sex.

This causes us to make irrational decisions. Are you truly in love, or dependent on the idea of it?

Many spiritual teachings imply the intellect and higher chakras hold greater value than the lower ones, and/or genitals. It's as if enlightenment only happens in the head, not the body. Religion has pushed God far away from us, up into the stars and inaccessible heavens. Our body is a temple for consciousness and can be used to self-realize. The original function of sex is not only to birth life but to experience our divinity and God. I feel sorry for all atheists having no one to talk to during sex.

Erotic stimulation will rouse sexual energy, the same creative force the Universe uses to create worlds. Although limitless in a cosmic sense, it's measured and finite in our bodies. Some mystics believe we only have so much life force within us before our body expires. They also believe our lifespan is measured by the number of breaths and heartbeats we expend. Every time a man ejaculates, he loses this vital life force. He does so unless he can learn to have an orgasm without spilling his semen. Women don't lose much through sex but do so monthly via their blood during menses. She gains energy from a man when he releases in her.

Younger men have an abundance of this creative force, yet are less able to transmute it. Having sex and masturbating are the easiest ways they know how to release it. A strong wind or a sexy statue will set them off. Older men have lesser amounts and need to preserve it, as it's more precious. They're wiser and know how better to utilize and redirect it.

Through the practice of Tantra yoga, both men and women can retain and recycle their sexual energy. Instead of it leaking outwards, it can be channelled up the spine to the higher energy centres and be used for spiritual purposes. Be mindful of how much you unnecessarily give away. Many limit sex to lust and carnal pleasure, which can be depleting. *Energy from an orgasm can be redirected for healing the mind, body and soul.*

Energy healers can feel and also manipulate one's energy. There's a ton of information encoded in it, just like a Wi-Fi signal transmitting through the air. You can't see it, but it's there. You may not be sensitive to energy, yet I'm sure you've experienced it when sitting or standing close to a stranger and got creepy vibes. When two people are close, there's a lot of information being shared energetically, via microbes, phero-mones, and non-verbally. Some believe women retain the DNA of every sexual partner she's had, as the genetic information via the sperm permeates and resides inside her cells, it can even cross the blood-brain barrier. Whether this is true or not begs one to consider who they absorb energy from. Is it good or bad? Guys should consider how often they masturbate and leak their precious life force. They also need to be mindful of who they're plugging in to.

You can tell how you feel after having sex. Do you feel em-powered or drained? Some feed off the energy of orgasmic release. The *succubus* and *vampire* are like moths to the flame. Those drawn to the light are the ones who lack it themselves; we seek what we don't have. What is your prime motive for sex; is it to feel a connection or just for pleasure?

## TWIN FLAMES AND THE TRAPPINGS OF SPIRITUALITY

Many years ago, I was in a spiritual bookstore and overheard a young woman asking for relationship advice from the store's employee. In her hand was a candle, it was a special one. She had asked if the spell candle could make her current *love interest* fall in love with her. I tried biting my tongue but failed miserably. "He has free will and the freedom of choice, I wouldn't mess with karma" blurted from my mouth. I knew the employee well, she smiled at me with a don't lose my sale face. I smiled back. This young woman like so many others, wastes valuable time and energy trying to morph guys into their ideal (fantasy) partners. They see their *potential* but destroy themselves in the process of trying to change or save him. They'll wait forever until it's too late.

Yes, many have potential and are good inside, but is it worth the time and energy trying to extract it from them? Chasing the little crumbs of hope only leads to constant frustration. Many overlook the red flags let alone the yellow ones, then act surprised when they get hurt, treated like shit and dumped. A high tolerance for disrespect means low standards and horrible boundaries, which is brought on by trauma and self-worth issues. Do you want to invest all that hard work only to have another benefit from it? Is that why you cling and won't let go? *Don't date potential, date reality.*

Ladies, guys are simple, *what you see is what you get.* If he does change, he will for himself, not to appease you. If he does change for you, it'll only be temporary. He'll become resentful and will almost always revert to his old ways. Some women are wounded healers creating trauma bonds in an attempt to heal themselves. *If a guy isn't ready, it's not your job to fix him.* Don't wait for him to change, unless you feel you don't deserve better. You can keep soothing yourself with comforting lies, or find someone who is available, ready and living their truth.

I want you to forget about twin flames, soul mates, past life connections and destiny. These notions are the very things preventing you from finding *The One.* You can cast every spell, do rituals, make vision boards, and perform all the law of attraction techniques you want, but they won't bring you what you seek. If they do attract someone, you'll probably fuck it up anyway. Why?

If you haven't done any emotional healing, one of you will run away, or sabotage the relationship. Forget the *runner* and *chaser* paradigm and all the dogmatic jargon of *twin flame unions;* if you desire such a connection you're most likely addicted to the hopium (hope + opium) it promises.

Whether you're the *chaser* or the *runner* is irrelevant; *a twin flame relationship is a codependency, a trauma bond in disguise."* Seeking your *twin flame/soul mate* says, "You're incomplete and looking for a saviour or something outside yourself to make you feel whole." This may sound harsh and burst your bubble, but I suffered from this nonsense too. Are twin flames real? Maybe, I don't know for sure. If you truly want to find your soul mate/twin flame, take off your mask and look in the mirror. Who would have thunk it was you all along?

Modern spirituality, especially the New Age movement, does more damage than it promises. It's a con job, a cunning deception that disempowers you from doing the required inner work for healing. Spirituality can be the ultimate bypass, a take no action, and this isn't my reality bullshit. You're passing the buck and refusing to take accountability for your crap. "Love and light" is another cop-out and deception. What happened to the dark shit you're hiding? You're neglecting the darkness because you're afraid to face your shadow, which keeps you enslaved to it. Whatever you do to avoid it is escapism, *a diversion.* You will need to face both your dark and light aspects.

Until you have done your shadow work, love is just an illusion. It will be a mirage and the source of your suffering—the bane of the love you seek. You'll keep attracting and blaming toxic partners until you figure it out. Being available and open to receive a healthy relationship not only requires healing and raising your vibration but also understanding masculine and feminine energy. *Polarity* work is essential for healing and integrating your repressed shadow.

## YOGA PANTS CRYSTALS AND DIVINE UNION

In the process of doing spiritual work, many women find their *power* and unleash their inner *Goddess.* They have many Goddess warriors to emulate: Athena, Freya, Kali, Macha, Joan of Arc, and so on. These powerful women have become the mascots of the modern female empowerment movement—the new matriarchy. Also, through spirituality, men find their *hearts* and get in touch with their softer side. They wear beads, crystals, and become *passive* touchy-feely *yes-men.* I was that guy and even took up yoga in the hope of meeting such a Goddess. There were many times I wanted to ask that beautiful woman doing a puppy dog pose in front of me out for a date. Due to the fear of rejection, I didn't. *Yoga pants are a gift from God and a thing to be admired.* I tried not to stare like a creep or *downward dog.* If I did happen to connect with a goddess, I'd lose sight of everything and float up into the clouds in a daze. I believed these women wanted a man like me, but sadly they only saw a SNAG; soy boy.

Our masculine and feminine energies need to be balanced, but the process of integrating them can make a mess of things. Men incorporating their feminine energy and women their masculine often create *imbalance* or *inversion.* Spirituality has taught me invaluable lessons and insights about myself and my connection to the universe. Also how to journey up my spine through the lower chakras and connect with the higher energy centres. I even learned how to identify, navigate and release trapped emotions I held in my body. But like most spiritual guys, I got stuck at the heart chakra and on higher levels of awareness. Although this may feel safe for women initially, it quickly becomes dangerous and unreliable. Women aren't attracted to this. My feminine energy became dominant and I lost my power to attract. I realized I couldn't stay where I was. I had to come back down into my balls and reignite the fire in my cock.

The Hindu tradition views the Divine as a perfectly balanced combination of male and female energies. They are represented by the *masculine Shiva* and the *feminine Shakti.* It's by the merging of the two that enlightenment is obtained. These teachings state there are three facets of Divine masculine energy which are represented by: *Brahma,* the creative force—*Vishnu,* the sustaining force, and *Shiva*, the destructive force. Brahama is paired with the creative Goddess Saraswati—Vishnu's consort is Lakshmi, the goddess of prosperity, beauty and abundance—Shiva is paired with the Trinity Goddess Parvati (she's the most complex aspect of female divine energy who's represented by Durga, Kali and Lalita. The main representation and culmination of male and female energies are typically represented by *Shiva* and *Parvati.*

According to Greek Mythology, humans were created with two faces on one head. We had four arms and four legs. Our early versions were strong, and the gods feared our power. It worried Zeus, so he split us into two parts. In the beginning, there were three parents: the *Sun, Moon,* and *Earth.* From the Sun was produced *Man,* the Earth *Woman,* and the Moon, the *Androgyne.* These severed Man-Man, Woman-Woman, and Man-Woman forms yearn for their other half. Ever since, we've been condemned, in the search for our other half. Is what we call love simply the desire and pursuit to become our whole?

Regardless of what the myths imply, there's no doubt many of us feel a deep yearning to connect with another to complete us. *This is the illusion.* In the physical world of duality, this may be true. Spiritually, we're pure energy and genderless, not split, severed or incomplete, *energetically* we are both male and female. In the flesh, we become polarized and governed by our biology. The desired union is for re-remembering or awakening our other half aspect, which remains dormant. It's also to connect with the creative force and Source of all that is. I once heard a spiritual teacher say, "Men have been created to coax out the hidden *reason* in women, and women have been created to coax out the hidden *emotion* in men. The purpose of the spiritual path is to balance and integrate both aspects. Yet this desire kills attraction between men and women.

If you want to pursue a spiritual path and strive to integrate both masculine and feminine energies, then go for it. Celibacy is better suited for you than a relationship is. By doing so, you're aiming for androgyny or sexless expression. The path to God is singular; the merging of the left and right eyes integrates the single third eye. You can have both, but to enjoy the duality, you'll need to polarize yourself. Do what you want in your meditation chair or on your yoga mat. But if you want to play in the sexual dance of the physical world, you'll need to become Don Juan or the gypsy Carmen; *and not a monk or a nun.*

Interestingly, I've noticed many on the spiritual path are single or questioning their relationships. One or both have grown apart, or their energies don't jibe any longer. Conversely, only when both partners have done *spiritual work*, is when they can enjoy both a *sexual* and *divine* union. So, what type of relationship do you want? Are you realistic, or do you escape into fantasy?

# CHAPTER TWO

# TYPES OF RELATIONSHIPS

## THE SIXTY-SECOND ROMANCE

Have you ever heard of the sixty-second romance? No, got a minute? Unfortunately, this is how long passion between couples lasts these days. If people would only commit to working on their marriage as much as they do planning their wedding then most would thrive. Many couples don't know the difference between a healthy and an unhealthy relationship. When I'm referring to the *types of relationships,* I'm not talking about marriage, common law, girlfriend/boyfriend, FWB, same-sex, swingers, polyamorous, or whichever. I'm not referring to their labels but to their dynamics. You are either in a *polarized relationship,* or you're not. This is the core teaching of this book and hopefully, you'll understand it by the end.

One day you're in paradise, on a tropical island with your soulmate and the next you're in prison with your cellmate. Your once-loving partner is now ordering you around like a jail guard. After a few days on the fantasy island resort, the food at the all-you-can-eat-buffet starts getting predictable, repetitive and boring. Yesterday's dinner recycles as tomorrow's breakfast and sometimes even lunch. We are led to believe the honeymoon doesn't last forever and it's normal for passion to fade; for the conventional relationship, this is often true. You may think the post-nuptial happy dance only lasts for those lucky ones who have found their person. Ironically, in the beginning, we all believe we're that couple until we're not.

You meet the love of your life, and the sparks are flying everywhere. But eventually, reality hits and you return to a place of mediocrity, a situation you said you'd never settle for. You accept it because it's normal, and you love this person. No one believes this collapse is their fault and will blame their partner for not caring or trying hard enough. They probably do care, or once did, but neither understand what's truly going on.

You've tried everything and realize there's no use carrying on. Eventually, one or both of you start pondering the cost of leaving or staying in the relationship. *"Is this partnership better than the hell I was in before? Will I be happier being single? If I leave, will I miss this way of life, the double income and social status? Is this lifestyle worth compromising my happiness, soul, health and peace of mind for?"* Selling out for a materialistic lifestyle while your soul is dying is never worth it. I'm not advocating divorce by any means, it's a painful experience. You were once madly in love and it's worth rebuilding if you can.

Sometimes we grow apart to the point of not relating anymore, and that's okay. Just don't ditch the car immediately when the engine light comes on. Try to work it out before you chuck-it-in-the-fuck-it-bucket. People aren't disposable, there are feelings, and children are often involved. There's no use going to relationship counselling if both partners aren't on board. A bird can't fly with only one wing; it takes two to tango as they say. Throwing seeds into the ground while expecting a beanstalk to grow overnight so you can climb up and get the golden egg is equally extreme. You still have to climb the vine into the clouds and avoid the giant. Great things take time to unfold and your patience will reward you. One has to wait nine months before holding their baby for the first time—then even longer as they watch them grow into adults and have children of their own.

## CONVENTIONAL RELATIONSHIPS

Did you know marriage is the leading cause of divorce? That's why some avoid wedlock altogether and bypass being another statistic. Not everyone wants to endure the three *rings of marriage*: the engagement ring, the wedding ring, and the suffer ring. I'm guessing you bought this book because you don't want to add to the ever-growing database. Maybe you feel you deserve more than just a mediocre relationship or wanting to ignite the one you already have, or save what's left. If you're married, you may admire single people and they may feel the same way about you. Are we ever truly happy? Whether you're hitched or not, we all want to have the best possible relationship, and avoid toxic ones. The question is, "Do you want a conventional relationship or a polarized one? You need to be clear on which type you want. I'll explain both and you can decide.

In a conventional relationship, the woman is usually in control, the man typically follows and is acquiescent, and he's afraid to stand up to her. He's reactive and waits for her to tell him what to do. Guys in these types of relationships are sycophants who attempt to keep their women happy. "Yes dear, no dear, how high do I jump?" Happy wife happy life? A happy spouse is a happy house may be true, but if she's the leader, he will feel unhappy and castrated. If mama ain't happy ain't nobody happy is another sham, she's your woman, not your mama. You don't need her permission to be a man. It's is no fault of the woman, she'll naturally assume control if he can't.

Women in conventional relationships can easily manipulate their men by using those famous *words: fine, nothing, go ahead, whatever, that's ok,* and *wow.* Some men take them at face value and feel assured everything is fine... until she torches his car.

Predicting the stages of a typical relationship isn't rocket science. In the beginning, both are drunk with love, two love birds on cloud nine who can't get enough of each other. Love goggles blind us against all flaws, quirks and caution flags. If one does catch a glimpse, they'll just pass it off, or figure it's something that can be dealt with later. No one cares about the pending hangover while imbibing alcohol the night before. Our ego won't let us look at our BS, so why would we bother to notice another's?

After a few months to about a year the love cocktail wears off, and our prefrontal cortex (critical thinking) comes back online. We notice our angel *has horns* and wonder, *"How didn't I see that before?"* All of a sudden you hate how they breathe and how loudly they blink. That nice behaviour and superhuman tolerance begins to wane, and you turn into a passive-aggressive asshole or bitch. I'm not being a pessimist, some do experience happily ever after. But not without *dedication, patience* and *work.* Their grass is greener because it was cared for and fertilized with lots of shit.

Then there comes the power struggle where differing views, beliefs and core values get challenged. The one with the stronger mindset wins and this can last three to six months. In the case of my parents, the battle never ended because both wanted to be in charge. Next is the trust-building period, allowing your partner to have a boy's or girl's night out. Trust eventually deepens but faith now is required to let your partner go on trips without you—the all-girl getaways and the fishing/golfing trips for the boys. We don't know what's inside the safe until it's opened. Until it is... faith is all we have. This is when trust and jealousy are challenged, and quickly expose themselves. Are they cheating, or are you?

Eventually, you figure out what's truly important and you know what you both want. You learn to let the stupid shit go and realize no one's perfect; the nagging and complaining aren't worth it. Finally, you get to the stage where every flaw is known and accepted. Maybe not all of them, but most. You figure it's par for the course; everything considered, you've got a good thing going. You know what you have and don't anticipate any surprises... *you hope.* You let the petty stuff go and deal with the major issues as they arise; you get through it. If you can survive all that, then mature love establishes. You become a team who grows together and helps each other—which then develops into *unconditional love.* This may be interrupted by a death of a spouse or child, an affair, loss of a job, or an illness. The choice at this point is overcoming the crisis together… or ending the relationship.

## O'DEATH DO YOUR PART

Many don't make it till death do us part, and a few take it literally. Some look for an escape clause or decide if the twenty-five years in jail for murder is worth it. You can only be on your best behaviour for so long because when the clock strikes twelve the facade collapses. You let your guard down and comfort sets in, then you start taking things for granted. Eventually, everything rises to the surface, so why camouflage who we are at the start? I'm not suggesting picking your nose on your first date, or shamelessly passing gas during the movie following. Or maybe that's the secret, *just be you* and let it all hang out right from the beginning. Let me know how that goes. The more inner work we do on ourselves, the quicker the relationship can evolve. Jealousy and mistrust won't be as noticeable, or problematic.

Going beyond the *surface* and delving into the *psyche* is where the real challenges lie. When her true motives surface, she becomes less adaptable and starts trying to change him. He begins to get lazy and his clothes somehow start missing the hamper and end up on the floor. Petty stuff arises, divergent habits, patterns and preferences begin to clash. The bathroom battle begins; is the seat left up or down, is the toilet paper in the mullet or beard position (over or under), is the toothpaste squeezed from the middle or the end, is his beard hair left in the sink or her hair-balls in the shower?

The war then moves into the kitchen battlefield. Who cleans the dishes, are they piled up in the sink? Who loads and unloads the dishwasher? Are drawers and cupboards left open just a crack, or wide enough to split one's head open? Things that didn't bother you before now begin to drive you mad. Even stuff you once loved about them will make you want to kill them. These are trivial issues indeed but are indicative of a deeper sickness growing under the surface.

We go into relationships with certain expectations; in the beginning, all may seem fine. Then, when the dust settles, you begin feeling buyer's remorse, and you want to sue for false advertising.

Guys get into relationships for sex, and women have sex to get the relationship. Thus, women control access to sex, and men control access to the relationship. She marries and *hopes to change him...* he doesn't. He marries and *hopes she stays the same...* she doesn't. Resentment sets in and begins to corrode the foundation both believed was solid. Needs stop being met and neither feels appreciated anymore. Both feel taken advantage of; it's all give and no take. Communication stops and huge fights begin. This breakdown is the *result* and not the *cause* of the real problem.

Subconsciously, you start using guilt and the same manipulation tactics your parents used effectively on you. That *passion* and excitement you once had now turns to *frustration*. You feel needy and hurt, old traumas and wounds surface. You stop having sex and blame the other for being the problem. The yelling gets louder until you both stop listening. Disrespect is dished out mutually. She begins to nag and bitch because he does nothing and sits lazily on the couch, and he tunes out. Resentment builds and you begin growing apart. *Any relationship with disrespect eventually becomes abusive and toxic.* You take each other for granted; you blame, criticize and deflect responsibility for your part. You wonder, *"How the hell did we get here?"* Instead of addressing things head-on with accountability, one or both start using diversion tactics. Things like drinking more and other *numbing, distracting* and *dissociative* behaviours.

If the sex becomes boring or non-existent, you may try to spice things up by kinky role play or experimenting with a swinger lifestyle. You bring in the turbo vibrator or indulge in more porn. He's sleeping on the couch downstairs and she's texting a dude in another room while drinking her evening bottle of wine. Harmless vies for attention can lead to innocent flirting, then into text affairs, emotional cheating and then sometimes... the real thing. Good friends notice your unhappiness and ask you what's wrong; you *lie* or *confide* in them. They're often worse off than you are, but you still listen to their bad advice. The drinking increases so does the complaining; you joke about how men and women suck. Time apart may seem like a good idea, so you take a break or go on an all-boys or girls trip.

Absence may make the heart grow fonder, but it can also tear it apart. You've been taught to stick it out, so you do whatever it takes to stay together. *Loyalty isn't what keeps you in a toxic relationship, unhealed trauma does.* You become despondent and stop trying to fix your relationship. You may end it and hope the next one will be better, but you realize it's always the same shit... just at a different address.

## NAGGING AND COMPLAINING

If I had a nickel for every time I've heard men and women complain about each other, I could have bought an island. While you may believe it's normal for couples to complain regularly, I disagree. The odd disagreement here and there is fine, but not when it's constant and no one listens to each other. Being a hairstylist for most of my life, I've heard it all; the same old shit regurgitated over and over. People pay tens of thousands of dollars for personal and couples counselling, legal fees, alimony and divorce. Hasn't anyone figured it out by now? I could have bought a larger island and added a yacht had I become a divorce lawyer. Sadly, in the early punch-drunk love days, no one thinks they'll end up hating or fighting with their partner. I know I didn't get married to argue or plan my divorce. I never understood why my clients never spoke to their partners the same way they confided in me. So many problems would have been avoided and resolved. Why are we so afraid to communicate?

While retaining my stylist/client confidentiality, I'll share some *fly-on-the-wall* complaints I've heard over the years.

WOMEN: he's never there for me, there isn't enough intimacy and connection, all he wants is sex, no foreplay, he cums too fast, he checks out other women in front of me, he gets angry too easily, he's a slob, his dirty clothes are everywhere, he doesn't listen, he smells, doesn't shave or groom enough, he doesn't spend enough time with me, or the kids; he doesn't help around the house, he thinks BBQing is preparing dinner, he can't communicate or tell me how he feels, he always watches sports, he doesn't know how to dress, doesn't understand or appreciate how hard I work, he doesn't compliment me on my appearance, doesn't notice when I get my hair done, he doesn't support me emotionally, he plays too many video games, he drinks too much, he can't get it hard anymore, he's reckless with money, I'm raising another son... and on it goes.

MEN: she nags and complains too much, she's too emotional, she wants to change or control me, she expects too much, she overreacts and her moods are over the top, she's controlling and bossy, she's unpredictable, she doesn't put out anymore, she spends all my money and blowjobs are a thing of the past. I could have stopped at nagging and no sex, but that would have been a typical guy thing for me to say.

In all seriousness, men are simple, we have an on-and-off switch. Women have a multi-gauged control system. I understand guys have fewer hormonal processes going on; women have to deal with a whole array of chemical reactions. She's too hot, too cold, hogs the sheets in bed and freezes him with her cold feet.

## MEN WANT TO BE HEROES BUT END UP ZEROS

Do you know why the bride and groom are always smiling in their wedding picture? He's happy because she gave him a blow job the night before, and she's happy because it's the last one she'll ever give him. Thus I believe why men coined the phrase, "Wedding cake makes women frigid." A client once told me, "I've been happily married for twenty years" his wife interrupted, "Speak for yourself." This is probably why women end marriages *three times* more than men do; they're more sensitive to marital problems. Statistically, guys experience a higher marriage quality and satisfaction than women. After my son was born, I remember my former wife saying, "Your life hasn't changed at all, and mine has!" Optically, men appear to give up less in marriage and as fathers. Today, more women have higher workloads being moms and having a career, while also tending to domestic duties.

Women want successful men, but many don't realize dating or living with such men can come with a price. There's a reason why a man is successful. Unless he's hit the crypto or lottery jackpot or fell heir to a family inheritance, the majority of his energy is directed elsewhere and not on her. He's always working and hardly at home. Many successful men possess narcissistic behaviour which they need, this drive and focus help them land the next big deal. As a result, she may find herself feeling *alone* and *neglected.* She often interprets his dedication to work as an obsession.

There's a danger for men to stop doing *the things* that got them the girl in the first place. In his mind, he believes the courting job has been done and now must address the bigger challenges. His current focus is to provide, make money for the family, pay the mortgage, fix the roof, and so on. In his mind, he's *raising the bar* and in hers, he's *neglecting her.* She misses the little things he used to do that made her fall in love with him.

She feels disregarded and retreats; her resentment grows, and she stops putting out. Women need to feel loved before they want to have sex. Since guys view getting sex as being loved, he interprets this as *she has stopped loving me*.

As a result, both feel rejected or neglected and may stray to feel loved and appreciated again. If she cheats, he's devastated and can't understand why. It's usually for a more energetic and sometimes younger guy named Chad. He's angry and confused because he has sacrificed everything for her. Now the asshole is driving his car and having sex in his house... *in the marital bed, he paid for.* Adding insult to injury, he loses everything in court, financially and time with his children. No wonder he becomes bitter and angry at all women in general.

Men usually fall harder than women during a breakup. They also don't rebound as fast. This doesn't apply to assholes as much as they've already moved on and are banging other chicks. The good guy is who suffers the most. Men typically don't have the emotional support system women do. They can't hug their friends or teddy bears, or cry on their buddies shoulders and share their emotions the same way she can. Men generally keep their emotions in and are taught it's weak to express their feelings. When women break off a relationship, they've been planning it for a while. She has been talking about it with her family and girlfriends before she pulled the trigger. She may even have another guy lined up. Guys are blindsided most of the time and are usually the very last to know. In contrast, I've heard horror stories of men plotting the same, hiding money and suddenly losing their job—from making six figures to flipping burgers.

## BAD SEX

There are many reasons why relationships fail. They range anywhere from a lack of communication, a betrayal of trust, too many differences, money issues, unwillingness to work things out, and even divergent cultures. I believe this all stems from dwindling attraction, *which is due to an unbalance in polarity.* The relationship becomes androgynous, lacking in intimacy and extremely passionless. This leads to the elephant in the room... *bad sex.* How often do you hear people say sex isn't everything? Do you truly believe that? Try telling an Italian food isn't everything. Maybe those saying it don't know how to cook well, or never had great sex. They don't know what they're missing.

Great sex is what keeps toxic partners from splitting up, it's also what keeps them coming back for more, even after many destructive breakups. I believe sex is the glue that holds relationships together. I'm sure you've had a toxic lover who you knew was bad news but kept going back because you couldn't get enough of them. It's like junk food. How many times have you dumped someone because of bad sex? For the majority of married couples, mediocre sex is common. Sadly, some have stopped having it altogether. They're simply coexisting with their partner, they've become roommates, TV companions, and travel buddies who do stuff with each other. Some are just allies raising a child together; yes, they've had sex at least once. Many couples live these types of lives and have settled for it, and that's okay. As long as it's mutual and there's no resentment.

Does this sound like a satisfying relationship to you? Is wanting more selfish and unrealistic? Well, would you rather have lots of great sex, or settle for nooky that's blasé and seldom?

What kind of sex do you want, one from being a byproduct of a relationship? Sex being an outcome of a relationship can be very good… or extremely bad; you get what you get. But a relationship built on passion is much more desired.

I believe sex is one of the strongest expressions of polarity, it's more intense in a polarized relationship. Great sex is the result of having chemistry, it doesn't create the polarity, it's the result of it. In a typical relationship, this is rare. *You can't start a fire without a spark.*

So, is it possible to have an amazing relationship that's forever in the honeymoon phase? Absolutely!

## A POLARIZED RELATIONSHIP

Envision a partnership with mutual respect for one another, filled with passion, great sex, clear communication, and little to no fighting. What would it feel like to have a successful and sexcessful union? Imagine a remedy to every problem and complaint a typical relationship faces. By learning a simple concept, this can all change. The theory is easy, but explaining and integrating it is the challenge. This needs to be experienced to fully appreciate what it is. We've been conditioned over many years, and change doesn't happen overnight, it's a work in progress. When applying what I'm sharing in this book be patient and continue to work on it. We all have wounds, limiting beliefs, distorted programming, self-worth issues, and insecurities.

The honeymoon drug only numbs these ails temporarily, as the euphoria wears off, the pain comes back online. We get discouraged because we have failed to escape what we have tried to avoid. As a result, the wounds come back even stronger. Unless you address what you're trying to avoid, you'll forever be chasing dopamine highs that desensitize you through affairs, toxic relationships and thrill-seeking behaviour.

A polarized relationship has been anchored when a man is in his *masculine energy* and a woman is in her *feminine*. When they both honour each other in this way, he feels respected; she feels valued and heard. He's inspired to lead and protect her, she's open, in her heart and able to receive his devotion. There's no desire for her to *control, nag* or *blame* him because her needs are met—she feels *safe,* at *peace, cherished* and *loved.* She knows her *vulnerable expression* is enough and trusts him to listen and to honour it. In doing so she amplifies and clarifies his leadership so he can better serve her. She'll feel the freedom and safety to *just be,* to create and express herself without any anxiety or pressure. She does not need or have the desire to control or manipulate him because he's got his shit together.

More trust is required in a polarized relationship than in a conventional one. Although I'm not into Bondage Discipline Domination Submission Sadism and Masochism (BDSM), I respect the rule of the *safe word.* Yet, I never understood how it could be *audible* through an orange ball gagged in someone's mouth. *I digress.*

A woman needs to express herself whenever she feels unsafe in any situation; the guy needs to be sensitive to her needs and concerns. Submitting to his leadership is a choice she makes alone, it's never forced on her. She can withdraw whenever she feels unsafe. She's free and can change her mind at any time. When a man takes control, he can't blame his woman because he takes full responsibility for making the decisions. She can't nag and bitch because she's trusting him to successfully sail the ship.

In essence, she hands him the keys to the car and lets him drive. But only if he displays healthy dominance and strong leadership. She has to *trust* him and *feel safe enough,* but... he has to earn that privilege. She's not going to get in a car with a drunk person—especially if she's ever experienced an accident; she'll be too traumatized to get in. *She'll want to drive.* When a man *leads* in a relationship, it's not for his ego, he's doing it for her and himself. He's not doing it to control or disrespect her, but to serve in total devotion, and to make life easier for her. In conventional relationships, women rob him of what he naturally wants to do, to *serve.* They deny him the very thing he thrives on. She feminizes him, and he no longer feels he has any purpose left; his devotion to her stops. He tunes out, or worse, cheats to feel important again.

Men and women have only one love language, he wants to be *respected,* and she wants to be *cherished.* A guy gets his needs met when his woman receives him and is grateful for what he offers. He feels respected, and loved; she gets her needs met and also feels loved. She radiates when what he offers her is given without her leading him to do it. If this section triggers you or seems foreign, I understand. I'll do my best to clarify it. I trust by the end of this book, you'll have a better *innerstanding* of what I'm teaching.

## SHE WILL NEVER SAY NO

I remember hearing the most enchanted words I've ever heard from a woman. She said, "You own me, do whatever you want to my body, I will never say no to you." It sent chills up my spine. I puffed my chest out like King Kong. When a guy knows his woman is deeply invested in him like this, he'll do everything in his power to protect her, and her heart. Nagging, complaining, doubting and challenging him in any way will do the exact opposite. He'll feel disrespected and won't be inspired to do anything for her. Similarly, when she knows he's all in and devoted, she can let her hair down, relax and enjoy life. "I've got this babe" are the most desirable words she loves to hear. If she's still resisting, then she doesn't trust him enough to lead her.

I know boss women who do it all or lead in their relationships. They take no shit and have little time for men who challenge them. I also know many single mama-bears in the same boat. This behaviour usually stems from necessity or is imposed on them by their upbringing. No matter how strong and able a woman like this appears, secretly she's suffering, and wishes someone would take charge and lighten her load. Unfortunately, she has no choice because she believes there are no men capable of stepping up. She's too afraid or unable to trust and forego her need to control. The irony is she's pushing away guys by the very thing she's compensating for. In her defence, lots of men have dropped the ball and can't handle it when she gets overwhelmed. Weak guys blame her for being neurotic and will gaslight them when they can't lead. They don't realize they're responsible for her so-called *drama*.

If you're still with me, that's awesome, but if you're ready to throw this book away and incriminate me, I'm okay with that too. Pass this along to someone who's ready to improve their relationship and love life. This material isn't for you; maybe past experiences have had a hand in this. You may have been bamboozled by fairytales, society and irrational narratives. All I ask you is to give me a chance to explain polarity and how it affects relationships. *Submitting to his leadership* may have also triggered you. We tend to react based on the past and limited information. So before concluding... hear me out. Why not read this as a comedy and laugh your way to the end? There's no reason why it should trigger you, unless, of course, there are unhealed wounds in need of attention.

## SINGLE AND FED UP?

Don't be upset if you're still single or not in any type of relationship. This is great news, because you have the advantage. There's no need to sand down and re-stain the furniture. You have a fresh canvas to work with. Healing a toxic relationship or one on life support can be lots of work. Sometimes it's unsalvageable and not worth the time or effort to undo all the hurt, resentment, and betrayal; it's hard to regain trust once it's broken. You're also in a position to consciously choose what type of relationship you want to experience. Having said that, the universe usually decides *what we need* regardless of *what we think we want.*

If you've done inner work, you'll quickly notice which flags to watch out for. You'll know if you're a match or not. You will move on if things don't feel right without even having a second thought. You won't create any drama, or try building a relationship on quicksand. Sadly, we hold ourselves hostage with our ignorance, and we'll repeat the same lessons until we learn them. *What kind of relationship do you want?*

Let's dig into some reasons *why you* may still be single. Then I'll share a few of mine.

# CHAPTER THREE

# WHY YOU'RE STILL SINGLE

## WHY ARE YOU SINGLE?

Are you sick and tired of being asked, "Why are you still single? You're beautiful and a great catch." They might as well say, *"What's wrong with you?"* Funny, it's a weird thing called standards, you may have heard of them. This is right up there with asking a woman why she doesn't have any kids, as both can strike a nerve. *"How about fuck off and mind your own business, I don't need to be constantly reminded by rude, nosey and inconsiderate people like yourself."* Oops, was that my inside voice? You try to be polite for the most part, and sometimes it's even comical, but after a while, the pressure can be too much to bear. Maybe they're just envious that you can be happy alone, or subconsciously they may be rubbing it in—it can feel that way sometimes. They're probably miserable in their relationship and are simply projecting. Maybe they've chosen to settle, or feel undeserving of having something better. Many are jaded and don't believe there are better options available.

If you're happy being single great, just stop trying to justify why you're so bloody happy about it. Are you trying to convince yourself, or others? There's a difference between being alone, and feeling lonely. Some can't stand being single and will settle for whoever is available. *I'd rather be alone than wishing I was.* I don't know many married women who say they'd get married again if they were divorced, or if their husband got hit by a bus. Everyone has their reasons why they're *alone*, but have you stopped to consider what yours are?

"I have a type and haven't met my equal yet, I want someone who gets me; I'm out of their league, good-looking, independent, confident and strong, so no one approaches me because they're intimidated, I won't change for anyone, others are jealous and sabotage my relationships; I'm cursed or paying off karma from a past life, I'm broken and unlovable, I don't need anybody, I'm happier alone, I prefer my freedom, it's too much work; all the good ones are on backorder, out of stock, damaged, married or gay."

Before you can heal, you need to become aware of your BS first, then you'll see it in others. Eventually, you'll realize we're all full of shit. I can answer the title of this book by saying, "You're too picky, ugly, you smell, are overly nice or too set in your ways. Your marriage sucks because you put up with it, or hope it'll magically change all on its own. You don't want to put in the effort, are afraid to stand up, feel undeserving, or you're stuck in the blame-complain-I'm-not-gonna-listen-to you spin cycle." Okay, we can all go home now. Seriously, we both know there's more to it than that.

## CHAD, STACY AND THE SEXUAL ECONOMY

Personal reasons aside, there may be a harsher reality at play. You could be the victim of circumstances that are out of your control. I'll be referring to some of the terms used in the red-pilled dating community. I'm not a member nor condone the dogma it disseminates. I recently dipped my toe in to see what was going on, I left these types of online pickup forums many years ago. I find these sorts of groups breed misogamy and misogyny. The men there appear angry and most likely have been hurt by women, and the sexual triumphs of other men.

The following are examples which depict this community's stereotypes. They may or may not be accurate assessments. Some are playfully extreme, so take them with a grain of salt. I don't prefer using labels or categorizing people, however, they're a good reference for identifying patterns and anticipating human behaviour. On some level, we resemble a few or all of these archetypes. Don't take anything personally, but if the shoe fits...

Meet *Chad*, a sexually active *Alpha-Male*, who comprises the rare top percentage of all males. He's the good-looking jock/bad boy every woman wants to sleep with. Then there is *Brad*, he has average looks and is considered *the typical dude*. On the bottom rung is the *Incel*, the involuntarily celibate male. I never knew about this term until Monday, April 23 at 1:24 p.m. in 2018. In my hometown of Toronto Ontario, a twenty-five-year-old man drove a rented white van along the sidewalk on Yonge Street and killed ten people; then attempted to run down sixteen more. Incels generally hate The Chads of the world because they're having all the sex, and usually with the Stacys.

The *Stacys* are the hot, long-styled hair, perfectly applied makeup, Gucci bag-carrying women who the Chads are banging. It's not only the Alpha men who desire Stacy but so do the sea of beta males who orbit them. Stacys will cuck every Brad they're dating until a Chad comes along. This behaviour can continue well into her forties and beyond. Many are entitled and expect special treatment from guys. Interestingly, they're quite submissive to the Chads. Some have had botox, their lips injected, breast implantation and often don't work (or hold down a real job). Yet, they seem to be living the life of luxury. This is thanks to her ex-boyfriends or wannabe's, and the beta male orbiters who subsidize her lavish lifestyle. She'll be the one most likely to have an only fans account and prey on the desperate Incels, and make a killing off of them. They're also social media influencers thirsty for more followers. Stacy is not a fan of the other and *lesser type* of women.

The *Beckys* are those who have the natural look and believe most guys prefer that. Ironically, she will be the chick sporting the crazy hair colours. She wants to bang the Chads too and will seek attention by wearing sexy clothing, or yoga pants. Becky may even post provocative pics online to draw awareness to her. Yet, she tends to wear loose or baggy clothes to hide her small tits and flat ass. She'll most likely work at the trendy coffee shop, or spend hours there on the laptop she pulls out of her cheap backpack. She'll have a few beta orbiters and white knight friends who'll support and defend her strong yet naive opinions she posts on social media. Beckys are likely to be feminists and usually need to be the dominant partner in their relationships.

The *Sexual Economy* states that only *twenty percent* of men are having *eighty percent* of the sex. So for every ten girls getting laid, just two guys are banging them. This leaves the *eighty percent* left to fight over the remaining *twenty percent* of the women. Many Stacys complain of male scarcity, but since they only go after the *twenty percent,* they're creating their own problem. Chads have the pick of the litter, why would they settle on one girl? The Incels struggle at the bottom and fantasize about the untouchable Stacy, chasing the more accessible Becky, and if they're lucky, settle with a *Femcel,* (a female incel). This is more reason to find a long-term partner and let all the beautiful people have fun while they can.

## I'M HOT, WHY AM I STILL SINGLE?

If you're fortunate enough to have won the genetic lottery and fall into the Chad or Stacy class of humans, then I congratulate you... *for now.* My condolences are forthcoming. Being one of the chosen, you may have noticed having greater opportunities socially, financially and sexually. Beautiful people get more attention and encounter favoured bias over the average folk. This may or may not be true in your experience, but studies have shown even mothers favour their better-looking children. Fair or not, this is a reality. Receiving special treatment regularly becomes normalized and expected, it's taken for granted; no longer seen as a privilege. It's all fun and games until you *hit the wall,* and the freewheeling is over.

The *epiphany* may come beforehand, but it's usually too late by then. You may not be one of the *beautiful people* but perhaps just as picky. You've been hitting the snooze button far too long... times up. Before you know it you feel old, sad and alone.

You believe you've missed the boat, but you didn't. Your ship came in, but you were waiting at the airport. You had a whole fleet arrive waiting in the harbour just for you. Don't worry, there's still hope, the front doorbell rings and you go to open it. Six little kittens are sitting in a cardboard box labelled '*Cat Lady Starter Pack*'. That's alright guys, you still have your porn and vodka to keep you warm at night.

Whether you're a single Chad or a Stacy, the reason *you're alone now* is that you screwed up. You're not a victim, you had it all, but you were *selfish* and made the *wrong choices*. You were reckless and rode the carousel of fun and casual hookups. Now you're bitter and hiding behind excuses. You refuse to take responsibility for any of it. Do you have any regrets, sad *The One* got away? You probably bookmarked them for later while you were playing the field. You weren't ready, were you? You misused your power when you had it. *Sorry, not sorry.* Don't get me wrong; sometimes life does deal us a bad hand. But you have to be honest with yourself... you fucked up and took things for granted. You only chased the hotties and ignored all the normies clustered around you.

How did you use your ten years of power and glory? Did you use your *assets* wisely? How many good guys have you friend zoned? The ones who were invisible to you, who'd do anything to make you happy. Instead, you chose the Chads who treated you like shit and didn't want anything from you... except for your pussy. Maybe you chased the white-collar dudes over the hard-working, dependable men who valued family and always came home after their shift. What would your friends say if you were with an ordinary guy? How many hearts of good women did you break or take advantage of? How many did you pump and dump because *you knew* there were more options cued up and waiting for you? You mistook *contentment* for *unhappiness* and *boredom*; *toxicity* looked like *excitement* because you had wounds and were unable to know what healthy was. You were looking for love in all the wrong places.

## CHECK ENGINE LIGHT

Most cars depreciate over time, and very few hold their value. Although some are worth more for longer, eventually all will end up in the junkyard. Some women still expect top dollar for their dwindling merchandise. Social media and desperate guys drooling over filtered pics falsely inflate their value; making them believe they can shop outside their price range. Studies show at *twenty-three,* women are at their peak attractiveness. Between the ages of *eighteen and twenty-five,* the world is their oyster. They have the power to choose almost any man they desire. Sadly at *forty,* even Stacy can't be as demanding as she was in her early twenties. Some women *hit the wall* even in their thirties. Although they may still be beautiful, their sexual value is compromised. I didn't say it was fair. Nonetheless, many women at this stage are like recovering junkies; they know they have to be more realistic and settle down, but can't help it and want one more hit. They'll go after another emotionally unavailable Chad who'll use them and they'll get hurt... again.

Women's empowerment tells you, "Have fun when you're young. Don't settle down, you don't need a man or a relationship. Go chase your career." Guess what? Unless you're a stripper, the career will always be there, but the guy and family won't be. Sadly, you may have it all now and you're finally ready to settle, but have no one to enjoy it with. You're beautiful and independent, your car and condo are paid off, you've made good investments, you have a bachelor's degree and make good bank, yet you wonder, "Why am I still single? Where are all the good guys?" Unfortunately, this is common, and you're not alone. It doesn't matter how beautiful, successful or independent you are; the truth is, most guys don't care about your success or your stuff. If he did, he wouldn't benefit from it anyway. Women falsely believe men are attracted to the same things they are. This mindset leaves many unable to find the men they think they deserve.

Like the old saying women tell men, "What's mine is mine, what's yours is also mine." Guys don't want your cash or your boss-woman attitude. *You've been lied to.* Unless he's a beta male content on having you support him, real men don't want you to be his *nurse* or *purse.* You've convinced yourself being single is not your doing, or the right guy just hasn't come along yet. Yes, a real man can handle an independent and opinionated woman, but he doesn't want to. A man wants to come home to a woman who won't bust his balls or someone he has to compete with. He just left a work environment full of competition. He wants a soft, agreeable, graceful, and less opinionated woman who isn't so career driven.

Also, waiting too long for marriage can cause *panic and desperation* to set in. This makes women more apt to *settle for a lesser man,* and for making the wrong decision in choosing a husband, or a father for their children. I've seen it time and time again. The longer women wait to settle, the faster their child-bearing window closes. *The biological clock is ticking.* There's also the potential for more complications during pregnancy. Conceiving could further be problematic, which can lead to needing a surrogate, adoption, freezing eggs, or an expensive IVF procedure. You may choose not to have a family now but may regret it later. No kids mean no grandchildren, and in old age this can be quite lonely.

## THE TABLES HAVE TURNED

God has played a cruel joke on us. At *eighteen*, guys are hyper-sexual, and can get rock hard in seconds but will cum before their dick is out of their pants. They're immature and haven't established any value yet. Many don't have jobs or money to offer a woman. They're at a disadvantage until they get older, mature, have stability and have made some bank. The *rub* is their plumbing may not work as well as before. Contrarily, women have the upper hand when they're younger. They have the looks, the power to entice, and are most fertile. She reaches her sexual peak by her *mid-thirties* to her early *forties*. She knows her body more intimately and can explore it without the guilt, shame and hangups that plagued her in her youth.

She has *more choices available when she's young*, and *he does when he's older*. Veteran guys can be pickier and are the ones putting women in the *friendzone*. Emotional intelligence ripens for women in their *twenties*, for guys it happens in their *thirties*. However, males and females are equal during their sexual maturity. Boys have their first wet dream around the same time girls experience their first period.

If a woman does meet a top *ten percent* guy, he'll most often overlook her and choose younger. Why? Because he can... and he knows his value. Men are more visual and naturally gravitate to women who are youthful, nubile and more fertile—*younger, hotter, tighter.* Naturally, this pisses women off, they're angry at the double standard. Males get more hate as they don't experience this reality as badly. It doesn't seem fair that men can age and not get judged as harshly as women. Some women become bitter or give up, this only pushes guys away even further. Man *bashing* isn't going to interest any guy.

They say men age like *wine* and women spoil like *milk*; you can't fault men for wanting to choose dairy prior to the *best-before date*, it's in their genes (jeans). Even *equality* touting Hollywood spits out their aging actresses to make way for younger and more beautiful *twenty-something* starlets. During my hairstyling career, I've done hair for many beautiful actresses, and I've always heard the same story, "Why isn't my agent calling me anymore? All I get cast for these days are to play matronly women." Sadly, many have gotten plastic surgery to stay relevant and to compete with the younglings. Some were only forty years old. If this happens to the stars and supermodels, what odds do average women have?

Guys also suffer delusions of grandeur, they *hit the wall* too. I had a *seventy-five-year-old* male client who still thought he could go out and pick up young hot chicks. He was balding, had a distended gut, was hunchbacked, wore soiled clothes and didn't have a penny to his name. He wanted me to make him look like a rock star. On his first visit, he showed me a pic of a young Bon Jovi and expected me to replicate his look. *"These are scissors buddy, not a magic wand."* With his government assistance cheques, he hired young prostitutes to get his fix. There was a big problem, and I'm surprised he told me. Testosterone replacement therapy and Viagra no longer worked for him, so he resorted to injecting his penis with chemicals to get hard. He told me the escorts would freak out when he took out his needle and syringe. It had to be done within minutes of intercourse so his dick wouldn't go soft.

I met another older client at a nightclub, he tried picking up a young woman. She resisted, and he countered, "It's not about age baby, it's a spiritual experience." Although age is just a number, it's also how you feel and how your image looks in the mirror. Some days our body can feel like it's *sixteen* and others, a *hundred and six*. Accepting our age and its limitations can be a hard thing to do.

## DUST BUNNIES

I was once on a dating site and read a profile with the heading, *"Dust Settles I Don't."* At first, I thought it was funny, but then I realized how indicative this was of what's wrong with everything in the dating world today. You can ignore those dust particles all you want, but when left to settle, they'll morph into bloodthirsty bunnies that'll bite you back into reality. *Settling* holds a negative connotation as it comes with the condition of a *sacrifice*, or you've got to *give up* things you don't want to. It's more about being *flexible* and making concessions.

Entitlement is rampant; we want things without earning them or offering any value in return. It's all take and no give, there's no reciprocation. No one wants to invest in themselves, or take accountability for their behaviour. We want what we can't have, we're too picky and believe we have all the time in the world. Whether you think you're God's gift or are hiding behind a thin veneer of false confidence to cover up your unworthiness, guilt and shame… *time is running out… fast.* Are you not settling because you know your self-worth or because you're afraid others will see right through your facade and call you out? We judge others but don't see our flaws. The ego is like a one-way mirror, it looks through the glass and feels superior while it hides behind the illusion.

We're afraid to commit to others and connect only on the surface. We don't build a solid foundation before bouncing to another opportunity. We're like polar bears jumping from one floe to another. Eventually, these icecaps melt, and we end up drowning…

I sure did. I was afraid to go deep with anyone, let alone follow the white bunny down the rabbit hole. Instead of settling, I became a delusional Chad who chased Stacy. I learned the art of pickup, which gave me unbelievable confidence. Pickup techniques do work, but only temporarily. They bypass a woman's defence system, mimic alpha behaviour and hijack her attraction switches. These techniques are manipulative and superficial, which may land you a big fish, but the victory of the catch will feel empty and unfulfilling. Hiding behind unrealistic expectations kept me safe, but each successful capture led me to more depression and feeling like a failure. I didn't settle because I was afraid to fail *and of not being good enough.*

## EXPECTATIONS & CONCESSIONS

Inflation not only affects money, it also influences *Sexual Market Value* (SMV). Today, many average-looking women believe they're worth more than they really are. Many dating coaches are now quitting the business because they can't believe some women's entitlement and unrealistic expectations.

Their standards and shopping list are so unattainable even Jesus wouldn't qualify. When these women finally find an eligible guy, he's usually not interested or wants a commitment. These matchmakers will find the perfect guy, but there will always be something wrong with him. Women who expect a top percent man usually have nothing of value to give in return. They believe having a vagina is all she needs. Last I checked, (as of 2021) there are 3.9 billion women (49.58% of the population) in the world; that's a lot of available pussy.

Many women think they can change a guy's mind. The truth is, he's either into you or he's not. If he was, he'd be all over you and would never leave you guessing. Ladies, stop wasting your time and energy; go for dudes who really want you. Guy's the same for you, quit chasing the hotties and supermodels you have no chance with, or you'll end up like my client injecting boner drugs into your dick. Just because a woman smiles at you doesn't mean she wants you, she's just being polite. Always take mixed signals as a no. Your ogling, cat calls, super likes and "You're hot" social media ass-kissing will not get her attention. Placating will only pump up her ego while lowering your value.

The irony is, the older one gets the less they'll settle, and sadly, the lower their value becomes. The solution is to change your must-haves and utopian non-negotiables into *preferences* and be more *flexible*. Even if you find your unicorn, there will always be something wrong if you look for it. Or, you'll quickly get bored of them. Before you demand the best of the best, ask yourself, "What do I bring to the table?" We've become so picky and full of ourselves—it's keeping us alone. My advice is to *lower your standards*. Now before you challenge me, let me clarify.

Absolutely *yes* to *no*: alcohol or drug-addicted manboys living in their mom's basement without a job or car, struggling with undiagnosed mental issues who are in and out of jail scumbags. These aren't the types of concessions I'm referring to. Lowering your standards means shaving off a few inches from your minimum six-foot-plus guy, and finding happiness with two or four-pack abs instead of six. I'm not saying to settle for a guy with a double-sized keg who says his belly is due to a backed-up cock, or is a gas tank for a sex machine. There is a shit load of great guys who you overlook because you're hell-bent on Chad. Check your friend's zone, there are hundreds of great guys waiting for you. I guarantee it. *Ya but... they're boring, too nice, blah blah blah.* These guys can *get laid* anytime as well, they just need to lower *their standards* enough. Guys, get past your supermodel-threesome-Barbie Doll bullshit. When she says she's *bi*, it may not mean *bisexual*, but *bipolar*.

Studies show as women age, their chances of finding a stable long-term relationship decline dramatically. In her *thirties,* her chances fall to *fifty percent,* in her *forties,* it's *twenty percent* and in her *fifties,* it drops to just *six point two-five percent.* By the time she hits *sixty,* the odds go down to a mere *one point six percent.* These are scary statistics. Since women's SMV peaks at *twenty-three* and men at *thirty-five,* we need to strike when the iron is hot—and when *we are too.*

All is not lost, and I won't joke about having a house full of cats, vodka, porn, hand lotion or a box of facial tissues. Work on yourself and I don't mean just physically, that's what has gotten us into this mess in the first place. I'm not saying to let yourself go because physical health and looks are still important. If you're truly humbled, take the time to self-reflect, and quit holding out for Chad or Stacy, then *you can and will* find your person. You have to do the inner work and stop bypassing. *Compassion,* a *beautiful heart,* and yes, a great *personality* work wonders. I believe a genuine *smile* on a woman is the most beautiful thing ever. Work on all the traits you didn't think were important when you had a hardbody; in your prime. As we age, the rules change.

## IT AIN'T WORTH HIS INVESTMENT

Marriage is a woman's insurance policy. Even if she gets divorced she'll still get something, in most cases more. Women take a chance when they get knocked up as free agents. Without a contract, many will be left struggling as single baby mammas. But behold, they can marry the government for support. Guys are learning it's not worth committing to marriage when they have so much to lose through a divorce; whether it's financially, their house, or time with their kids. In many countries, women have no place to go if they leave their husbands. They may know he's out whoring around but will settle and stay for the security the marriage affords. In the West, single mothers have more opportunities after a divorce. Is this why they are the ones leaving the marriage *seventy percent* of the time? Guys will even take care of another man's child and give up more to make their women happy.

At one time, men controlled their wives from seeing their friends. Today, more women are placing those same demands on their guys. Men are also losing the friends and freedoms they had before the relationship. Dudes also need space and will feel smothered if stifled, and that is why they'll often retreat to their man caves or garage.

Ultimately, feminism is hurting women and preventing them from what they instinctually want; love, family etc. Their message is, *"Fuck like a guy whenever you want, be free and independent."* Ironically, this benefits guys as this removes any obligations for marriage or commitment. Just like women don't want to buy the pig for a little sausage, he doesn't want to buy the cow when he can get the milk for free. Why should he invest when he benefits without buying in? Guys once had to earn the right to have sex with a woman. Now it's served on a silver platter, this keeps guys in Peter Pan mode; there's no need to mature.

If women want to act like guys, why would men want to be with them? A man seeks the benefits a real woman provides, like her soft nurturing and graceful demeanour. He'd rather be alone than with another guy he has to compete with. Men will sacrifice themselves and give the shirt off their backs to women who appreciate them—he won't to those who break his balls.

Single moms can scare guys away. They don't want to be ATMs or raise another man's kids. They don't want to endure the brunt of their anger towards their baby daddies and from the guys who previously hurt them.

So what's left over for the decent and hard-working Brads after the Chads and toxic guys have run through and decimated these women? The answer is complex... and for another time.

## SMOKE SCREEN

I once heard a woman say, "I want sex, but now I need to feel a connection. What's wrong with me?" We still have needs, but as we mature, sex becomes less physical and more about mental and emotional contact. You may not even get aroused if the vibe isn't right. Welcome to midlife and the trappings of maturity. You may have been a master at playing mind games with others, but now you've become a genius fooling yourself. Do you self-gaslight into believing you need to be alone for a bit? Do you need to take a break? You're single by choice and better off alone, right? This may be true and you may actually need time to sort things out. *Is that the real reason?*

Alone time forces us to question why we have trouble in relationships. We can go on the proverbial dating detox and swear off courting for a while—we can adjust our expectations and find ourselves... then what? When the self-inflicted purgatory is served, do you honour your new wisdom, or do you go back to Chad and Stacy chasing? Do you test your luck and take another kick at the can? Do you believe it's different this time? Do you run the same old programs hoping you don't experience another break-up or divorce? Or do you finally get it and shift? Are you truly ready and emotionally available for an authentic relationship? Have you cut all ties with your past lovers? Do you still have unrealistic expectations?

# CHAPTER FOUR

# WHY I WAS SINGLE

## SEEKING PERFECTION

I had to be honest with myself and figure out why I was single after my marriage and common law relationships. I wasn't happy going to events, everybody was paired up. I was always the single guy. Why did I look at couples with envy, yet whenever I found someone, I'd find something wrong with them and want to break up? I'd look for flaws, and of course, there would be. Who the hell is perfect anyway? I sure wasn't. I was searching for my unicorn, not a bisexual woman willing to join me in a threesome, although, I wouldn't be opposed to that. No, I was seeking the mythical creature type. The hard to catch-rare-to-find-smoking hot-not batshit crazy-amazing sex and great personality variety. I was so busy looking for them I didn't see all the beautiful horses grazing around me. Until recently, I had a checklist of standards so detailed no woman had any chance of meeting them. Whereas in the past, all I needed was a nice smile, and for them to like me.

When in a relationship, my wish was to be single, when single I wanted to be in a relationship. I suffered from a yoyo-bipolar-want-what-I-can't-have-and-when-I-have-it-I-don't-want-it-anymore syndrome. I made sure my dream girl was unattainable, then I wouldn't have to be vulnerable again. If either of us caught *the feels or got too close*, I'd find any excuse to dump her. I'd be looking for an exit to escape, Shawshank Redemption style. I had a process for evaluating potential long-term commitments; I'd stare deep into her eyes and ask myself if I could look at her face forever. Could I deal with her quirks, habits and sounds? I'd imagine her getting old and wondered if I could live with what I saw. Then I'd start to feel trapped, smothered and wanting to leave before it got too serious. The thought of eating the same meal *day after day* freaked me out.

I didn't want to see my flaws, but she had to unconditionally accept me as I was. I could be shallow, but she couldn't. Was I just jaded, and trying to protect my heart from getting hurt again? Maybe, the answer was somewhere between being overly cautious and selfishly carefree. *Double standard much?* I was full of ego and believed there were no worthy women out there able to receive all I had to offer. When invested, I give everything and go all in, but whenever doing so, it was never enough. I knew my worth but was insecure at the same time. How could I feel self-important and be so self-critical at the same time? This dichotomy kept me frustrated, confused... and single. Why couldn't women see my value? Was I not in my power? Was I delusional? Maybe I chased broken women who couldn't see me, or were unable to receive what I had to offer. I vowed never to give any woman the power or chance to hurt me again, especially if they didn't have the capacity or aware-ness to value me. What was the use anyway?

I'd want women who didn't want me but had a line-up of those who did. I was not only a magnet to those in the queue but to married women as well. It was probably because they were safe, and I had nothing to lose. There wasn't any pressure to commit, which allowed me to be myself. Single women made me nervous; I would lose the ability to speak coherently or to think critically. There was more at stake... being vulnerable and getting rejected. Every rejection confirmed my feelings of un-worthiness. I chased smoking hot girls who could inflate my ego, but once I knew they were interested, the challenge was over and I moved on.

Those I wanted had to be *hot* and *intelligent*. If I could look deep into her eyes and see the back of her head, it was on to the next. I was after more than just their looks, I wanted some-one who had more to offer; beauty, brains and spiritual; well at least, open to my crazy beliefs. I wanted a woman who could go deep, who wants the cake and not just the icing, one who wasn't afraid to be vulnerable. A woman who has self-respect and high standards, who wouldn't settle for jerks, didn't com-plain, hate men, or still suffered from a wounded heart. She had to be emotionally available, ready to receive and okay with being alone. I didn't want a codependent partner, but one who chose me because she wanted me. I got very close a few times, but I freaked out and bailed.

I also hid behind the fear and excuse that after a failed mar-riage, a common-law relationship and losing two homes, *I was protecting myself.* Not wanting to go through the loss of financial and emotional suffering again was a valid excuse, right? Maybe, but was I going to hide behind that rationale forever? I played the victim and blamed everyone for my bad luck and poor decisions. To be honest, I didn't trust myself and didn't want to screw up again. When I fell in love, I got stupid, and things moved too fast. My father's famous words, "Son, you don't have to marry her because you slept with her." "Hold my beer, forget about marriage, I'm going to buy a house." It didn't take long before we were house hunting. Finally, I bought a house; me, myself and I. All three of us were very happy... but alone.

I realized the house I was single in for many years was never fully renovated. The upper hallway and steps leading to my bedroom needed painting. The drywall patching wasn't even sanded down, and this was *from when I first moved in ten years prior.* Even the plastic coverings for the light switches and power receptacles I removed to prepare for painting were absent. Energetically speaking, I was Gandalf declaring, *"Thou shall not pass!"* The path leading to my bedroom was uninviting. Maybe deep down I didn't truly want a relationship and preferred the freedom and safety of being single. Yet, I was still whining at being alone. It was *until* I painted and replaced the outlets that I allowed love the chance to enter.

## THE WIZARD OF CAUSE

I suffered from the four survival archetypes which is found in Joseph Campbell's *The Hero's Journey and The Wizard Of Oz* movie. They are *The Child, The Prostitute, The Saboteur,* and *The Victim.* Without getting deep into it here, they're represented by Dorthy, The Tin Man, Scarecrow and the Cowardly Lion respectively. These aspects are like the legs of a table that hold up our life and purpose. My innocent inner *child* always looked for *attention* while it struggled to be *heard* and *seen.* I was wounded and played the *victim, "Poor me, the universe is against me, it's not my fault."* Someone else had to fix and save me. I wasn't in my power. I feared it and didn't trust my potential. So I compromised and betrayed myself; and my values.

I *whored* myself by selling out for approval, not sexually but by being agreeable with everyone. This led to guilt and shame, thus destroying my confidence. It caused me to stay in and accept situations well past their expiry date. I *sabotaged* everything good in my life because I didn't feel worthy enough. It was better the hell I knew than the heaven I didn't. I'd even push away those who tried to help me. I was stuck in my *comfort zone,* feared change and didn't take any risks. Many times, I'd give up right before the pinnacle of transforming. Just like a worm only enters the apple when it's ripe, fear enters us when we are ready to change, or on the edge of a breakthrough.

The only way I truly healed was by moving through my fear and limiting archetypes. Bypassing them just made it worse. I had to do lots of inner work to release my childhood traumas, which kept me looking for the perfect mate; *the unicorn.* The more healing I did, the less I demanded perfection from myself and a partner.

## CLIMBING MOUNTAINS

When I was younger, I'd do whatever it took to find a girl. Even climbing Mount Everest wouldn't have been out of the question. As I got older that enthusiasm slowed, if not stopped altogether. After all the letdowns and efforts wasted, it was easier to wait for the mountain to come to me. Why can't I just tell the universe what I want and wait at home in my underwear until the delivery drone drops her off? If I'm meant to find her, it'll happen, right? Fate would find a way. There had to be a Soulmate Tracking System app I can download somewhere.

As time passed, I didn't want anyone interrupting my life, or having to drive more than twenty minutes to see. If I did, they'd have to be worth changing out of my sweatpants and showering for; worth setting aside time away from my work, hobbies, and writing. At this stage of life, my energy, freedom and time are precious. If I did connect with someone, they'd have to be okay with meeting once, maybe twice a week. I wasn't into constant texting or feeling the obligation to give them loads of attention either. They had to adapt to my schedule.

There's not only the energy expenditure but the time investment required to sift through all the *potential hopefuls.* What if it didn't work out? I'd have to start all over again. I had to deal with their drama, stories, financial obligation, bonding and possibly detaching from their friends and family members. That's a lot of entanglement to deal with. Then there's the expense of having to process the shared fluid, DNA and energy exchange I'd absorb through sexual osmosis. I didn't want to energetically take on anyone's guilt, anger, shame, trauma, spirit attachments and all that comes with physical and emotional intimacy. *I was a freak.* This is what spirituality and an impossible checklist can do to a person. It's also how the fear of rejection and being vulnerable can affect them.

I've turned down many beautiful women and have been accused of being gay as a result. If their energy didn't feel right or the vibe was off, *I was turned off.* So what if I got another notch

in my belt, after the orgasm then what? "That was nice babe…
now go make me a sandwich." Hookups are easy, but they're
depleting, selfish, gratuitous, repetitive and usher in spiritual
atrophy. If they didn't nourish spiritual growth, what was the
use? Eventually, fast food will make you sick. Instant gratification is like eating a bag of chips, you always want more and
you'll still feel hungry afterward. We do need carbs, but also a
balance of all the other macros like protein, fats and complex
carbs. My energy was better invested in someone who was in-
vigorating, not depleting. I've done casual but it always felt like
I was masturbating inside them. They were just a receptacle, I
didn't feel any connection.

Sometimes people get lucky and find their *forever person*, but
it usually takes lots of *time* and *effort*. Many don't want to invest
and would rather wait for the drone to drop them off. Being
single can get addicting, and once you taste the tranquillity of
freedom, dealing with other people may not be as alluring. I
got comfortable being alone, maybe deep down I wanted to be
single and not give up my independence. Yes, sometimes I'd
have to fend off feelings of sadness and loneliness as they crept
in, *but they always passed.* Once I accepted the 'toilet cleaning
laundry fairy' wasn't going to come, I became self-reliant and
responsible for my shit. I know newly single women who feel
like they've died and gone to heaven for not needing to clean up
after a man-child anymore. No more worrying about getting
their asses wet, or falling into the bowl because they know the
toilet seat is always down.

I questioned if I truly wanted to change for anyone, and
believed a partner would only complicate my life. I loved my

independence and didn't want to rely on anyone. I got shit done when I wanted and never had to hear about why it wasn't done right away; no deadlines. My bed could be made or not, and the dishes could be in or out of the sink. Still, deep down I craved a connection, so I slept on one side of the bed and kept up with the chores. I even put the *toilet seat and lid* down. I realized I needed to be game ready, *just in case.*

## EXPECTATIONS

Total surrender dissolves all expectations, and the ability to manipulate. When there's nothing left to lose, when the ego no longer has a story to sell or an identity to protect, and when rejection is all played out... is when one is truly open to receive without interfering. I reached that point, *or so I thought.* Secretly, I still had hope and continued trying to manipulate the universe; trying to convince God I was ready and open to receive what was best for me and not what I wanted or expected. I tried convincing myself I was destined to be alone forever and had to make peace with it. I believed it was fate and God's will because there was no way being single was my fault. *I was looking for His pity.*

I would say all the right things, "When you least expect it, it comes. When you stop trying it happens, the harder you look the harder they hide. When you don't need someone is when they appear. Like getting pregnant, it happens when you stop trying. Stop chasing the butterfly because you'll never catch it, when you least expect it, it will land on you. Have fun, enjoy life, don't be so eager... I'll meet her when I least expect it." I was lying to myself and pretending I was ready to receive whatever was meant for me *without anticipation.* I was delusional and gaslit myself, no wonder the Universe didn't respond.

I was waiting for the butterflies to take my breath away, for the sky to part and for the angels to sing. If I didn't instantly feel it with a woman, I'd move on to the next, or hold out until I did, which never happened. I was obsessed that I'd meet her at the next party, workshop or meet-up. There was always hope each time I deleted and reinstalled a dating app. I thought, "This time it'll be different," but it was the same old shit. I lost hope and convinced myself I was broken, cursed, or paying off karma from a previous life; *I must have been an absolute asshole.* I was jealous of how others could meet the *next one* so fast. Was it luck, or were their standards that low? Was I asking for too much? Were my expectations that insane? Why was it so easy for everyone else, but not for me? I deserved it and had suffered long enough. All good things to those who wait? *Pfft!*

Nonetheless, it was a constant battle between *click vs spark.* On the off chance, there was a flash, it always burnt out quickly, and when I clicked with them there was no spark. It became frustrating, it was a constant ping-pong match between the two. Damn it, why couldn't I have both? I had enough girls who were just friends and wasn't looking for another. I tried giving everyone a chance and looked beyond the *surface.* I had made every attempt to *connect and feel attraction,* with no success.

I discovered new ways of gaslighting myself. "It's because I've ascended past the lower chakras and have transcended the flesh." I've evolved, not easily tempted and I've seen my share of naked women. It wasn't a woman's looks that would sauté me into oblivion, but her energy. I didn't want a temporary flash in the pan or a lukewarm simmer. I wanted a roaring fire with lots of *passion* along with *friendship*. I finally convinced myself and made peace with the fact of dying alone, and willing to walk away from anything less than I deserved. *"Love would come when my standards were no longer negotiable."*

## ROOMIE

*"You have to keep breaking your heart until it opens"* ~ Rumi. I know you're a wise Sufi mystic and poet, but I don't want to fuck up again, my heart's been broken enough. *"Dear Frank, if you go around walking with your armour up and continue being defensive, how can anyone feel safe enough or want to enter? You'll never find true love with a closed heart."* "Dude, it was wide open, but it's not worth getting hurt anymore."

I became a master at *avoidance* and would *over-analyze* everything. I found every flag and non-negotiable possible, even ones that weren't there. It was like renting a car or a moving truck, I'd examine every line and mark, expecting to find a flaw, which of course I did. *If you go looking for snakes; you'll find them.* I found myself making excuses, cancelling dates last minute, and just about every other trick in the book. Fantasy stays on the other side of the veil, and so did my unicorn. It takes vulnerability, accountability and integrity to forge a bond that goes deeper than the surface, something my wounded self wasn't prepared to do. Since value isn't valued anymore, it was much easier to replace the void with a novelty item… until that drug wore off.

## BUTTERFLIES IN THE STOMACH

We all want to feel those *butterflies,* don't we? You know, those *magical feelings?* Sometimes I'd fool myself into believing I had found my person. The problem was, I mistook the fluttering as *attraction* instead of what it truly was… *anxiety.* If it wasn't there, then she wasn't the one and not worth pursuing. Maybe I was addicted to *fear* because I felt bored when it wasn't there. In nature, whatever is being chased after is called prey, and why they run. Perhaps those butterflies were signals for me to run, and my body saying, it was *overwhelmed* and *anxious.* Was I chasing after *chaos* and dependent on it to feel alive? If the hunt was too easy I didn't want it. Could it be I was uncomfortable with stable and normal? Did I interpret affection as a co-dependent attachment, something that just felt good? Was I addicted to it? What if I learned love wasn't safe, but something reckless, dangerous and unstable?

Wanting creates *resistance* which is repelling, it reeks of *desperation.* To want means you lack, it's saying I don't have it. We only seek what we don't have. Chasing isn't safe or attractive. Women could smell my *fear, neediness* and *desperation* like a wild animal. I became a *predator* and they were my *prey.* Have you ever noticed when you're in a relationship, you get hit on more? The neediness is gone. The moment you externalize what you want, you become the chaser and repel the very thing you desire. Until I learned to *become* that which I *desired,* I was pushing it away. When I stood in my power, everything I wanted was drawn to me like a magnet because it emanated from within me. If you don't learn this, everything you do becomes transactional, people will become a means to an end, to get your needs met. Instead of a place of *sharing*, it becomes one of *taking*.

## TIME ALONE & GOING DEEPER

By dating a lot of people we can learn about who we are. Each new person gives us a chance to reinvent or discover ourselves. Usually, we just get better at perfecting our bullshit. We recycle our best stories and routines, we play them back on endless repetition. Instead of allowing new experiences to refine us, we chase what we know, what's comfortable; and we stagnate. This is great for our ego, as it can fall deeper in love with itself. Ultimately, the real work is not to entangle with *many* people, but to remain and learn with *one person*. Doing so, all your warts eventually get exposed and your novelties die off. Shit gets real, and there's nowhere left to hide. Unless you find someone else to fool for a while. Eventually, all your hidden aspects arise. This process can deepen your love for another and yourself. This is hard work, but it's how true love will flourish.

A client once said, "If you ever date a musician or a standup comedian, never go to their shows. It'll get boring and predictable really fast and you'll begin resenting them." She was right, it's not easy hearing the same joke or song over and over without getting somewhat annoyed.

Society doesn't seem to place much value on *depth* as it does on the *superficial*. Hookup culture and instant gratification are more appealing than cultivating a deep connection. Maintaining morals and integrity takes *discipline, perseverance* and *commitment*. We can become addicted to the dopamine rush sex and a new romance give us. These relationships become transactional and a way to soothe our feelings of loneliness.

Only when every method to numb our pain has failed is when we'll seek help... or completely give up.

Whether you're single by choice or by circumstance, there's potential for deep insight, you're afforded time to journey inward. You're granted an uninterrupted opportunity for self-exploration and reflection free from the distractions and demands imposed on you by others. You're afforded the time to grow and uncover patterns undisturbed. This is much different than trying to find fulfillment by serial dating or jumping from one monogamous relationship to another. *I tend to avoid women who can't be alone. I don't want to be needed in a codependent way... I don't like sticky.*

When we've done the inner work, we can meet others at their level without judging them or having any expectations. We can be present and interact with them not from our stories or victim identities, but from our attentiveness. There's a knowing they're unable to complete us or make us happy. No one can make us happy, that's our job, they can only make us happier. We honour others and ourselves by not imposing that responsibility onto them. We stop being selfish and cease lying to ourselves. People are no longer seen as disposable or a means to an end. These pursuits are not desired at the expense of breaking another heart or adding more notches to a bedpost. We begin seeking true intimacy, which takes true vulnerability. We allow others to get to know *all of us*, both the good and the bad. This is unconditional love, knowing they'll still love us regardless of our flaws.

We learn that *love* and *sex* are two different things, it's knowing no matter how much sex you have, it's never fulfilling.

Promiscuity becomes a choice because sex is something you enjoy and not a way to satiate the emptiness gnawing inside you; *the starving void in your soul.* Sex isn't intimacy, anyone can get naked and fuck, but how many can get absolutely naked and truly expose themselves?

The way out is by going in. I know it's a cliche but I'm gonna say it anyways, "Happiness is an inside job." You need to rummage through the disregarded bones buried in your closet. If you don't, you'll just take the same skeletons to a different bedroom. I know this very well as I've spent many years being single and in and out of toxic relationships. I've learned from trial and error and have used my *alone time* to work on myself. I could have continued blaming and burning through a long list of women leaving a carnage of broken hearts. Eventually, one has to ask after their *sixth marriage* if they're the problem and not the other person. Are you ready to take accountability?

We're all on different paths in life, each has unique lessons to learn. You may be perfectly happy snorkelling on the surface admiring the coral below you. Or, you may need to dive deeper to touch the bottom of the sea; and look at the coelenterates and marine life up close and personal. There's no right or wrong path. What I've shared thus far may be enough for you. I'm offering an opportunity to go deeper down the rabbit hole... if you so choose. We've only scratched the surface of *Why You're Still Single or In A Shitty Relationship.*

Join me for the rest of the adventure. Let's look at what's going on in our society and how social dynamics are influencing our choices, behaviour and attitudes toward relationships.

# CHAPTER FIVE

# STATE OF AFFAIRS

## THE DECLINE OF MORALITY

The previous chapters covered our *reasons* for being solo or unhappily coupled. The next four focus on what's happening to us and society. Also, how it's affecting our psyche and early childhood conditioning. Morality is slowly eroding and is affecting our dating life, marriages and overall happiness. There are multiple reasons which go beyond the choices we make. Our preferences may be the direct result of social engineering. These factors can manipulate and override our natural tendencies; they are systematically engineered constructs designed to hijack our instincts. Are we the products of *nature or nurture... or both?* Are we being groomed like young puppies and trained to obey *authority* by those that don't have our best interest? Are we victims of an agenda with nefarious intentions? Do I sound like a conspiracy theorist?

The most coveted demographic for advertisers is between the ages of *eighteen to thirty-four*. This group is more receptive to marketing and is willing to *buy in* more than any other. If this social class is a barometer of where we're at in society, *we're in trouble.* Currently, over half of them don't have a romantic partner... *that's alarming.* Women have been taught they don't need a man and children don't need a father; *men are giving up.* We live in a hookup culture; there's a war on men and gender, *equality is misrepresented and distorted.* Marriage breakdowns are leaving single-parent kids home alone, in daycare, and left susceptible to potentially undesirable behaviour. The crumbling of nuclear families divides and weakens everyone, leaving them vulnerable to indoctrination. The rising cost of living, the need for a double income and the tax pirated on those earnings are *paralyzing.* As family values erode, *the system* waltzes in and become the surrogate parents. This keeps the biological parents powerless, divided and fighting with each other.

## PLUTO'S RETURN AND UNIVERSE TWENTY-FIVE

British military officer and historian Sir John Glubb wrote *Fate of Empires and Search for Survival.* He examined the rise and fall of all the major empires of the last 4,000 years. Bernard Goetz wrote *When the Empire Strikes Out* and used some of the material in John's book to point out the hallmarks of declining empires. Common patterns were found; the decline of sexual morality—an increased divorce rate—an aversion to marriage in favour of cohabitation—reduced birth rate, increased abortion, gay sex becoming publicly acceptable and spreading—increased economic and political power of women and the rise of feminism. I cast no judgment here. I'm simply sharing researched observations. Is all this due to natural and unavoidable cycles or by nefarious interference and fabrication?

I believe it's a bit of both as nature follows patterns and cycles. I've noticed the rise and fall of these great empires all share a similar timeline. Assyria, The Roman Empire, Britain and all the ones in between had an average duration of 250 years before falling. Interestingly, Pluto, the planet of death and rebirth (the great revealer) has an orbit of 248 years. The United States was founded in 1776, and as I'm writing this book the planet has returned. Pluto influences the *end* and *beginning* of new karmic cycles. Look at where society is now.

American scientist John Calhoun experimented by creating an ideal world using hundreds of mice; he called it The Universe 25 Experiment. Calhoun created this paradise of mice to mimic human societies and how they work. He designed a big enough space where every rodent had an abundance of food and water, and was free of predators. He started with four pairs of mice, which in a short time, produced a rapidly growing population. But after *three hundred and fifteen days*, it began to decrease significantly. When the rodent population reached *six hundred,* a hierarchy was formed between them. Larger and more aggressive rodents started to attack the group, and many males collapsed psychologically. Females stopped protecting themselves, became aggressive against their young and lacked reproductive drive. Simultaneously, there were lower birth rates and an increase in mortality in younger mice.

Interestingly, a new class of beta males appeared. They refused to mate with the females or fight for their space. All they cared about was *food* and *sleep*. Calhoun noticed two death phases with the majority of the new beta males and isolated females. The *loss of purpose in life* beyond a mere existence and no desire to mate or raise the young—they became reclusive. Eventually, all the young mice died, and reproduction dropped to *zero*. Even though the food was in abundance, cannibalism increased, and so did homosexuality. John Calhoun repeated this exact experiment *twenty-five* more times, and each time, the result was the same. I believe we are currently witnessing a similar societal collapse. Men are becoming more feminized with a decrease in protective instincts, and females are more aggressive and masculinized with decreased maternal instincts.

## SWIPE LEFT, MY COFFEE SUCKS

"Step right up and get your tickets here, try your luck and spin again." Carnivals and fairs may be on the decline, but not the exhilaration we feel when we attempt to win the ultimate prize. Life in those days was simpler. "Do you want your coffee black, with milk, sugar, or a double-double?" Thanks to designer coffee houses, those archaic menu options are a thing of the past. Now, you can select any type of roast you like: white, light, medium-dark, dark, or any of the other sixteen shades of the coffee rainbow. You even get to choose the beans: arabica or robusta and even how fine or coarse you want it ground. Do you want an espresso, latte, Irish, Turkish, drip, decaf (chemical or Swiss water method), or any of the other *twenty-plus types* available? Would you like soy, coconut, almond, rice, oat, or gasp... real milk added? Do you want it steamed, foamed, or flat? Do you prefer agave, honey, stevia, coconut sugar, maple syrup, baileys or grappa as your fix? Oh, it's not hot enough? Sure we can dump it out and make you a brand-new one. What's that, it's too hot and you're gonna sue us because you burned your tongue?"

You may think I got carried away there, perhaps, but I haven't even mentioned every coffee option available. So, what am I getting at? When our parents met, times were simple, as was their coffee. As long as the other person had two arms and legs and wasn't hideous looking, it was good to go. Marriage was *essential*, albeit *transactional*... it was uncomplicated. Prior generations were more committed to one another and they didn't have our cavalier views on commitment. Unlike today, they needed each other more so, granted social and economical environments were different. Things have changed since and we've evolved past the need to purely *survive and procreate*. We're now able to explore who we are and how we relate to others in a more profound way. With more choices available, we face a greater challenge of making the correct decision. Will we make the right choice? Is there something better waiting in the wings?

We've become so used to the drive-thru, instant gratification and no questions asked return policies, buyer's remorse is easily remedied. Unlimited variety coupled with available short-term lease options makes it easier to trade in or dispose of potential burdens and liabilities.

Relationships don't seem to last as long and are less stable than before. As familiarity and routine set in some get bored or suffer FOMO (the fear of missing out). They're curious to smell another's rose bush, or want to see how green the grass next door truly is. We have too many options and opportunities available.

Instead of pulling levers, we can spin again by swiping *left or right* without ever leaving the toilet seat. Hundreds if not thousands of prospects are queued and waiting for us in the palm of our hand. We have so many options we're unable to choose at all. We're suffering from *paralysis* by *analysis,* afraid to commit to anyone. We stay on the surface and never truly get to know anyone before we're back to swiping again. The stain doesn't get a chance to penetrate the wood and can be sanded off easily. We base our choices on the pics and bios stored in digitized human catalogues. Our interactions are carried out through texts, DMs and other *impersonal* and *misgiving* forms of *communication.* What happened to social interaction and going out for some java? Would you like your coffee black, or with milk and sugar?

## DOUBLE STANDARDS

We all have double standards, and there's no use denying them. We can fight this argument until the end of time without resolution. Women can hit men unprovoked, but men can't hit them, even in self-defence. Men can have many female friends but women can't have male friends without getting labelled. *"My kids are my world and you should accept them, but I won't date dads."* There are unlimited examples and *justifications* for both sides, but my beef is when standards become hypocritical, irrational, shallow and condemning.

We've been taught men are more visual and less judgmental than women are. I first thought this was true, but after sharing a dating app swipe session with a female client while her colour was processing, I was shocked to learn the truth. We switched phones for fun as it was a chance for us to explore each other's process of elimination. "He's too short, too fat, too this, too that, he has a cat," and on it went. *Wow, women are worse than guys!* So, I did some research and learned women *swipe left three times more* than men do on dating apps. I saw a study where both men and women were shown one thousand pictures of the opposite sex, all with varying body types. Results showed, men were attracted to *eighty percent* of the women across the board, but women chose only *eighteen percent* of the men who had a similar *body type.* Are men more balanced and accepting when it comes to how a woman looks? Women it seems, are more *selective.* Could this be due to social engineering, or have women always been like this?

Women are *praised* for having standards and men are *shamed* for them. If a woman turns down a guy over his looks, *it's her preference.* Yet, if a guy does it, he's considered shallow and judgmental. If he desires a fit woman with a low body count, he's accused of *fat and slut shaming.* Women live in a different reality than men do, for guys, it's harsher and unforgiving; this forces them to adopt a more realistic view on life.

I've noticed the majority of women's dating profiles are *devoid* of bios and information regarding their interests and personality. She can ask, "How tall are you?" but he can't ask how much she weighs. Her, *"It isn't the weight that defines the person."* Him, "Then neither should his height." Why's it *okay* for women to shame men for what they *can't* control, but *not okay* for men to express their preference for attributes women can?

Guys can't change their height or penis size, but women can control what they eat. There are several Big Beautiful Woman (BBW) dating sites available, but how many cater to fat men?

Imagine if I said I'd only date women who were 5' 6", had a BMI of 18, had blonde hair, blue eyes, D-cup boobs, had to have a thigh gap, flat tummy, hourglass figure, and a 0.7 hip to waist ratio? They'd call me shallow. Yet, it's okay for women to demand a guy have the four-sixes and to take a hike if he doesn't. I'm not talking about Satan's offspring, but a six-pack, six-foot, six-figure and a six-inch plus penis freak show. I understand if she's tall and would dwarf him because she chooses to wear high heels longer than his dick, but how often is she in heels? Sure they feel safer and protected with a taller guy, but when has height ever been a factor in making men smarter or become more ethical? Is this why most politicians stand at over six feet, and those who win elections are typically the tallest?

At 5'10" I don't fall into either the short or tall category, so I'm not bitter nor suffering from Napoleon Complex; heightism doesn't affect me. Having said that, short guys can be very strong; they have a lower centre of gravity (like a bulldog) and can be better protectors. I don't blame tall women hating on short girls for stealing the tall guys. Did you know only *twelve percent* of the world's male population is six feet and over? Ladies, go to the Netherlands if you want a giant, they have the tallest average in the world. In contrast, most guys don't care about a woman's height. Unless they have to step on a soapbox to kiss them. As my father used to say, "Height doesn't matter when you're in bed."

Women have been taught to hate sex, or at least to feel guilty enjoying it. This is of course changing, yet, those who have strong libidos are getting shamed for it. The double standard says, guys are respected for having a high body count, but not women; their value dramatically lowers. This is why some women weaponize it and call other women whores, tramps and sluts. Some associate sex to value and use it as commerce. They think if a guy pays a hooker to get laid, she can do the same. Why not get something out of it and use sex as a business? *Sex for resources.*

Since she has the goods guys want, sex can be used to control and manipulation. Some women have developed of sense of entitlement because they're simply alive and have a vagina. The hotter she is, the more worth she believes she has. Sadly, some give it up too fast, and believe it's their only value; this often backfires. Men with options won't respect her, and she's left surprised when he quickly moves on.

## DIVORCE & PROMISCUITY

Researchers estimate that *forty-one to fifty percent* of all first marriages will end in divorce; *sixty percent* of second marriages and *seventy-three percent* of all third marriages suffer the same fate. There goes the notion of *practice makes perfect.* Marriage among the young is also dropping off. How many couples are truly happy in the marriages that remain? Many stay for the sake of their kids, money, lifestyle, guilt, or to avoid getting judged by family and friends. WTF happened?

The Summer Of Love was in 1967 in San Francisco, California, where over one hundred thousand hippies joined together in celebration. "Make love not war" was the slogan; free love, group and communal sex could be found everywhere. It was an anti-war, pro-freedom and drug-induced orgy coalition; an experiment to cast off conservative social values. This changed everything, spawning many movements and protests between and after 1969's Woodstock; which attracted four times the amount of people. Flower power gave rise to girl power and opened the door to feminism. Women no longer wanted to be a wife-slave in marriage. Good or bad, change was happening. The rise of birth control pills, prophylactics, burning bras and feminist lobbying began to increase. So did STDs, abortions, religious backlash, and... *disillusionment.* Free love was misinterpreted as free sex and love without responsibility. There was heavy fallout.

Some believe LSD and the hippie movement were created by the CIA to get kids hooked on sex, drugs and rock and roll. Doing so, they wouldn't overthrow the Military industrial complex—it may have worked. Whether there was an agenda behind this or not, it happened... and began dismantling the once-stable nuclear family. Men became lazy or too high to give a shit about being protectors or providers. Women began embracing sexual freedom, empowerment and choice as men have before them.

This is evident today as the music industry showcases female stars sexually exploiting their bodies. So is the over-sexualization and priming of young girls to wear provocative clothes, and the trivialization of sex. The summer of love now entails our youth engaging in rainbows parties, wearing sex bracelets and sexting. Like inflation, the value of sex and marriage has depreciated. Statistics show that between 1933 and 1942, *ninety-three percent* of women were virgins before marriage. Then between 1963 and 1974, that number went down to *thirty-six percent.* By 2010, only *five percent* of new brides were virgins. Chaste women were mostly churchgoers and more religious than those who indulged often. The fear of going to hell, guilt and shame around sex for being an adulteress played a huge role in keeping themselves unsullied.

One study showed women with *ten or more* partners were *the most likely* to cheat or get divorced. Those with *three* to *nine* were less so, and women with *one* to *zero* partners were the least likely. Interestingly, women having only *two* partners had a higher risk of divorce than the *three to nine* group. Does fidelity correlate to the number of sexual partners women have? Statistically, it may seem so. You'd think curiosity would kill that cat having only one partner, but then again, you can't miss what you never had. I admire those who mate for life because the grass isn't always greener. The novelty wears off with everything.

Did you know, over *two-thirds* of all divorces are initiated by women? This number jumps up to *ninety percent* among college-educated women. Additionally, *ninety percent* of women are favoured in divorce court rulings. I wonder if these statistics would change if men had that same advantage.

## HOLLYWOOD

Movies and television *programming* are also big factors that influence *infidelity* and cause *divorce.* They've also contributed to the demoralization of family and martial values. Many studies show people mimic what they see on the screen. There is a ton of research on the link between onscreen content and risky behaviour, including casual/high-risk sex, binge drinking, fast driving, and even violence. Speeding and carjackings increased immediately after the first *Fast And The Furious* and *Gone In 60 Seconds* movies were released. I even went to play nine-ball with my friends right after watching The Color Of Money, a film about a pool hustler named Fast Eddie. People imitate the behaviour and language of the characters they find cool or have power and authority.

In 1930 a Catholic priest and the Catholic publisher of the Motion Picture Herald co-wrote *The Motion Picture Production Code.* This was commonly known as the *Hays Code,* which prevented films from depicting criminal violence, suicide, birth control, abortion, racial relations, homosexuality and divorce. The Hays Code ended in the 1960s; coincidentally, ten years later during the late 70s, films about divorce became very popular. As a child, I still remember watching Robert Benton's *Kramer vs. Kramer.* It gutted me and left an indelible mark on my psyche. I was afraid my parents were going to divorce. The 80s ushered in a divorce rate nearly doubling that of the 60s. Is it a coincidence it preceded another ten-year cycle? The movies weren't the only ones showing divorce, the celebrities were following suit in real life too. Whether you want to believe it or not, we are affected by what we see on the screen. Peer pressure and keeping up with the Joneses have the same effect—following the herd is human nature. I can remember when my friends were all getting married and having kids, it seemed like we all did at the same time.

## CHEATING

What do seahorses, sandhill cranes, grey wolves, barn owls, bald eagles, penguins, black vultures, beavers and swans have in common? They're all monogamous and mate for life. This begs the question, "Are humans naturally predisposed to fidelity?" *I don't think so.* If we were, there wouldn't be so many affairs and divorces still happening. Is marriage an institution created to keep us in line and to overcome our natural tendencies? I wonder if divorce and infidelity would increase if religion, guilt, cultural pressures and economics were removed. Would you cheat if you knew you could completely get away with it? Are we non-monogamous at our core? Does every relationship have an expiry date?

Do you believe once a cheater, always a cheater? The stats say those who've cheated before have a *three hundred and fifty percent* chance of doing so again. Can a relationship recover after infidelity? *I don't think so because trust is forever broken.* The betrayal will always fester in the back of the cheated-on's mind. If you had an affair or have ever thought about it, would you tell your partner? Should you? Which has the greater consequence, keeping it a secret or telling them? One will ease your guilt and the other will hurt them. A client once told me, "Never tell your wife you cheated. Even if she catches you in bed red-handed, tell her she's hallucinating." Another client said, "The secret to a happy marriage is to have a mistress. No presents, cards or saying I love you." I think the guilt would kill me and I'd have to come clean.

A survey conducted in 2016 showed *one in four* young cohabiting adults admitting to cheating on their partner. It went on to say only half confess, which mirrors the *fifty percent* divorce rate statistic. Interestingly, women admit to being unfaithful more than men, and more so if they were angry or seeking revenge.

When reality shows first began, I remember watching one where couples were sent to an island and separated from each other. Both were tempted by other hot singles. From that, I learned men and women cheat differently, and for different reasons. A man's betrayal is committed *physically*, and a woman does *emotionally*. Guys cheated because the opportunity was there, like a squirrel snatching a nut. Guys can have sex with other women and it can mean nothing; they can go back to their wives and still love them the same. When women cheat, it's at a greater cost, although not always, her relationship is typically done. There are emotions involved, so it gets more complicated. Her water is slower to boil, and so is her temptation. But when it happens, there's no stopping her.

Being a hairstylist, I've noticed which signs suggest a woman's imminent infidelity. There were drastic changes in appearance, which I was partly responsible for. Facelifts, boob jobs and considerable weight loss were the most common. The winner was when they asked me to cut their hair very short, partially or fully shaved. The kicker was when they wanted it bleached super blonde. I'd always joke and ask them, "What's his name?" I haven't been wrong yet.

In men, weight loss and an increased income give them carte blanche. There are no valid excuses for cheating regardless if you were angry, feeling neglected, hurt, seeking revenge, drunk, horny or just bored. Break up beforehand if you need to stray. Chasing dopamine highs elsewhere is an indication of deeper issues, ones you're avoiding and wanting to numb away.

Anything you can't do or say in front of your partner that you wouldn't want them doing behind your back is *cheating*.

Infidelity is not only committed through blowjobs and penetration, but also by heavy flirting, kissing, cuddling, and even sexting. You don't even have to touch another; sometimes, an emotional affair is worse than having sex.

How do you know if your partner is being unfaithful? Your gut will tell you. If you think they are, it's probably true no matter how much you try gaslighting yourself otherwise. If you sense it, you don't need a psychic to confirm it, *you need proof.* You can be pretty sure if they get angry or defensive when you confront them, or when they accuse you of cheating; *they're just projecting.* If they quickly become hypercritical, have new interests, change their routines and patterns, late evenings and unexplained whereabouts, have new sex moves or suddenly become interested in their looks… chances are high, they're two-timing. Another tell is when they suddenly become interested in your itinerary and track you 24/7. Since keeping up with lies takes effort, they'll tend to double-check by asking you if they mentioned certain things before. *"Hmm, I can't remember if I told you this lie, or not. My stories need to line up."*

If you have a joint bank account, watch for money being withdrawn; credit cards are traceable when paying for hotel rooms. The least obvious sign of cheating is when all your relationship problems magically disappear. This may seem like all is well, *but it's not.* When your partner stops confiding in you less, they've also stopped investing. If they start picking fights and blame you for insignificant things, they're trying to make you look bad. They need to justify their infidelity and a reason to leave.

When dating someone new, there are flags to watch out for. If they cheated to be with you, be careful, you could be next. Guys, if your new girl talks about her friends or family members sleeping around, or is caviller about cheating in general, she may be *hiding* something, or trying to *justify* it. Women don't usually cheat on guys they value; they do when they're not their best possible option. I'm not picking just on women, statistically, they cheat as much as men do. Girls are just better at lying about it and not getting caught. Affairs and one-night stands don't happen by themselves, they need two consenting participants.

# CHAPTER SIX

# ATTACK ON THE SEXES

## OFF WITH HIS BALLS

Is feminism attacking and distorting the *feminine*? Is it encouraging its demise? "Be a strong independent boss woman, provide and protect, sleep around and be free to do whatever you want without asking anyone for permission, especially from men. Your way or the highway, take it or leave it. You don't need a man, except maybe for the occasional dick, dinner and dinero."

If you're able and enjoy doing house renovations, repairs, twisting the lid off the jar, lifting heavy boxes, shovelling three feet of snow, and are happy with your vibrating pussy plunger, then you truly don't need a man. How's that working out? Are you happy, peaceful and truly enjoying your freedom? If you're honest with yourself and can honestly say that's the case, *congratulations...* you're one of the lucky few. Do you want to do and control everything all the time? It may well be out of necessity, but it doesn't have to be. Do you truly have it all? Is it really worth it? You've burnt your bras and have stopped shaving your legs and armpits; that's *awesome.* So, when will it be enough... and when does it stop?

I once heard a woman say, "We had it all, but we fucked it up. I could have stayed home and had the most rewarding job ever, raising children and making my house a home. Now, I gotta do three times the work and carry all the responsibility. Dammit, I'm fucking tired and burnt out! Meditating, drinking wine and doing yoga while doing the dishes isn't helping."

Ladies, if there is a man in your life, I wonder if he's happy in his submissive role. Is he lazy and mailing it in, or is he constantly at your service? Does he wait until you ask him for help—as he watches you do all the housework? Are you frustrated? Are *real men* those who need to embrace their feminine side more? Do they need to have their balls chopped off because they're too toxic and masculine?

It's not only men getting attacked; so are boys, girls and women alike. We've all been blinded by distorted truths, and our ignorance is being used as weapons to antagonize us. We no longer desire or care to see from another's point of view, it's only about us. It's always *the other gender's* fault for destroying our lives; the innocent who've committed no crime other than their unconscious incompetence and ignorance.

We complain about each other, but are we behaving like the kind of person they'd want to be with? Instead of blaming and criticizing, how about we stop deflecting our shit onto each other and start communicating. Why is it always someone else's fault and never ours? I believe this hatred has been engineered to keep us divided and destabilized, it preys on our egos and insecurities. Social exclusion, sexism, hostility, belittling, gynocentrism, patriarchy bashing and violence all need to be stopped. So does laughing at demeaning jokes and memes which promote the ridicule of men and women. If you're not looking for a solution, you're part of the problem.

Having said that, notice how *the solutions* are *never addressed*, it's always about *the problems.* We throw rocks at each other when we should be tearing into the social engineers behind this mind control; and those infecting us with the misogynous and misandrist viruses. Political correctness is weaponized; especially on dominant men who call out the bullshit. They're ostracized and isolated and so are the women who choose to be feminine and retain traditional and moral values. We all want things to change, but *no one wants to be the ones who do.*

## PRINCESS PROGRAMMING

Since birth, we've been assimilating corrupted programming, lovey-dovey stories and fairytales; we have boughten into romantic comedies. All have shaped our expectations towards love and relationships. These narratives have quashed our instincts and have cast unrealistic expectations of what *happily ever after* should be. Without this meddling, we would have figured it out naturally and would be happier for it. Instead, we've become casualties of these delusory fantasies and impractical expectations. That's why I prefer Shrek over Disney, as it was more realistic. The green rotund ogre and Fiona embraced their differences and imperfections; they wrote their own script.

Did you plan your perfect wedding at five? Did you wear your fanciest dress and mommy's oversized heels to marry daddy? Fairytales have duped you into expecting that someday a prince will come to save you and you'll live happily ever after. Once you learned about romance, love and flowers, you were well on your way to riding the magical unicorn up into the clouds. Most guys don't stand a chance to emulate Prince Charming, the majority are left *confused* and feeling *dejected*. You want a prince, instead, you get a battle-worn dude wearing chinked armour. Movies and cartoons have preyed on young girls who have fallen victim to the princess programming agenda.

Infant eyes and malleable minds are ripe for this early indoctrination. Look beautiful, seduce men with your gaze, let them pamper you and pacify them. Why? Because you're a princess who doesn't need to give anything back except for your beauty. This creates a shallow mindset and forces women to be obsessed with their looks, which of course, leads to insecurities. This is further cemented by fashion magazines and distorted images of celebrities; making women and young girls beauty slaves and lifers to the cosmetic and fashion industry. No man is ever good enough unless he meets *all of her standards.* Moreover, women are taught to crave security and money over a man's character. On first dates, I've never been asked if I've ever been to jail or if I loved animals and children. Neither, if I was a decent person with morals, or emotionally available. No, the first question was always, "What do you do for a living?" which always implies, "How much do you make?"

Security is essential, *yes*, but it's an illusion. We've been sold on its validity and permanence. *Safety sold by another is slavery.* The idea of freedom is dangerous; I'm not referring to real liberty, but the engineered type, which uses comfort as a weapon. There are two lions, one's in a cage and the other is roaming wild. One is afforded security, shelter, food and medical care; the other has no guarantees whatsoever. Which one is truly free?

Are you safer with a man who's strong, handy and can get stuff done? Or, with one who can't, but has the money to hire someone to replace the burnt-out light bulb, or have the drain unclogged? *The simplest of things.* One viewpoint is *taught,* and the other is *intrinsic.* Who can better protect and provide for you if shit goes sideways? How many truly happy women do you know who are bathed in luxury, that aren't struggling emotionally, or have an addiction to drugs or alcohol?

## THE DISAPPEARING MALE

Have you been noticing a recent and steady decline in strong, independent and self-aware men? It appears all the great guys are taken by the lucky girls; and the good-looking ones still available, are probably gay. These desirable males are being replaced by an overabundance of passively weak obedient little boys still living at home in mommy's basement. Spineless and out-of-shape man-boys have flooded the market.

In defence of most men, we've been manipulated and also carry inherited guilt over the ill-treatment of women throughout history. We're taking the fall for what the *'patriarchy'* has done to them. With or without justification, we also bear the weight of the *me-too movement* and the brunt of toxic masculinity. Sadly, women also feel disgraced for having contributed to what was perpetuated by these men. Guys are afraid to be masculine for fear of receiving backlash and being associated with the toxic patriarchy. As women are becoming more empowered, men don't know how to act anymore. They're judged when they act with *bravado*, and also when they appear *soft*. Most guys don't know how to handle stronger self-realized women, those who've become reborn after years of suppression. They're no longer *compliant*, or *submissive*.

Men will cower and attempt to satisfy these women, or try to gaslight them into doubting their sanity. This creates further division and madness. Just as asshole narcissists are making a bad name for the rest of us good guys, so are toxic bloodsuckers prostituting themselves are to good women. Some women take advantage of the legal system, blackmail guys and falsely accusing them of domestic abuse. We can't paint all men and women together like this. Most men want to work hard and provide for their women and family. The majority are not power-hungry sociopaths who devalue and oppress them. Men are afraid to lose what they have worked so hard to build. They can lose it all in one biased decision by a politically correct judge and get shafted in divorce court.

The legal system was put into place to keep law and order, but it has failed men and society. A man can no longer defend his rights and freedoms, or those of his family. In the past, when a crime was committed, the town's men used to band together and lynch the perpetrators. They'd protect women and children first and take matters into own their hands. The present system has handcuffed them. Here in Canada, a man can't even protect his family from an intruder without getting charged, no matter how dire the situation. The government has supplanted the *family's protector*. As a result, men have given up and become docile.

Similarly, in 1992 The National Hockey League implemented the instigator rule. This was to prevent any player from starting a fight. Instead, what it did was punish the enforcer protecting their star player against vicious cheap shots. As you may have guessed, the dirty players began taking liberties knowing anyone who retaliated was sent to the box. I believe the current system is doing the same. This is destroying masculinity.

## THE EVIL PATRIARCHY

Is the toxic patriarchy comprised exclusively of all straight males who have a dick and testicles? Or, has the term been created by a limited few at the top of the food chain? Are royal families with ancestral bloodlines, the controlling elite and tyrannical governments responsible for demonizing men; so they can stay in control? Most guys are *good* and want to do the *right* thing. Toxic patriarchy isn't comprised of the majority, nor the marginalized or dangerous men. Women are manipulated by this narrative and men are held hostage by it. There's an agenda created to *attack* and *divide*, not only against the masculine, but the *sacred feminine* and nuclear family. Who's left to defend the household from the tyrannical and coercive hyenas if all the male lions are gone?

Men having *privilege* and social *advantage* is untrue. Last I've seen, women are getting away with murder; they aren't charged equally for similar crimes committed by men. Awarded custody favours women *eighty-four percent* of the time; death by war affects *ninety-seven percent* of men, which is the same statistic for workplace accidents. Who risks their life on top of scaffolding hanging from forty stories high? Who connects the high voltage wires so the underprivileged can enjoy the luxuries of life? The evil patriarchy, or *over eighty percent* of the hard-working men who face death daily? Did you know homicide affects *seventy-six percent* of men, and *eighty percent* from suicide? Additionally, women have much more influence in society; *eighty percent* are consumers and *sixty-four percent* vote. Yet, men are shamed and attacked. Do you feel any *vitriol* towards me for mentioning these facts?

I'm not denying women weren't burnt at the stake for burning a man's steak. Unfortunately, many innocent women were *set ablaze* and tested by being thrown into lakes with stones tied around their necks. Most died by fire or from accidental drowning (if they didn't float up fast enough to prove their innocence).

Why have men throughout history blamed women for all their problems? Pandora opening the box, Eve biting the apple and every story depicting women causing havoc. Medusa was even punished for getting raped by Poseidon, then cursed by having her hair turned to snakes, which turned people into stone if they caught her gaze. Yet, many Goddesses/Priestesses such as Isis, Ostara, Ishtar, Parvati and others were worshiped. So what happened? Did these potent women abuse their power too? Did they become *'the toxic matriarchy*? Have we gotten to a similar cycle in history where women had power over men? Has the pendulum switched sides and is now against men? Have males become the new target, now being demonized and attacked?

Men were once threatened by wise women or by those who could heal. They oppressed and controlled them in fear of losing their dominance; whether this was intellectually, emotionally, spiritually, or of course, sexually. Even today, men who can't handle strong women will either cower or become domineering and tyrannical in an attempt to control them.

I find it ironic how some countries are in favour of concealing a woman's femininity with clothing, while others encourage it by the removal of it. Do you agree with full coverings, or skimpy clothing and bikinis? One approach attempts to discourage sexual temptation, the other encourages it.

*Guys seem to be very respectful towards half-naked women frolicking on the beach. They only stare at the covered parts, not the skin.*

## FEMINIZING MEN

Does being a *man* involve watching porn, drinking booze and becoming a muscle head? Men are sold lies, like those that claim drinking alcohol is masculine; it actually reduces testosterone and health. Drinking beer with the boys increases irrational thoughts and encourages *childish* behaviour. Not to mention what steroids do to a guy's balls and internal organs. Excessive porn watching and masturbation reduce a man's ability to sustain an erection and will lower his testosterone; *sex drive.* Furthermore, he won't understand what true intimacy is or what type of sex women truly desire. Real women don't look or fuck like they do in porn. Look at how the fashion industry shames the masculine by promoting shaving and no body hair. They humiliate men by putting them in dresses and high heels to strut down the fashion runways. Men are taught masculinity is toxic and chivalry is condescending.

This is all held in place by sitcoms, funny commercials, cartoons and movies portraying men as bumbling and incompetent fools. The plethora of chemicals in our food, water and grooming products are raising estrogen, lowering testosterone and disrupting the endocrine system in men. Women in the meantime are encouraged to be more masculine. As a result, men counterbalance by feminizing—to uphold the balance of polarity. This is a vicious cycle because when men don't man up, women are forced to, *and masculinize.* When one polarity is strong, the other changes to compensate. Nature is always trying to find its balance.

Men are also socially engineered to *appear masculine*, but their masculinity is bred out of them and replaced with *masculinized* behaviour. Things like fake machoism, confidence and the objectification of women. They're no longer protectors who fight against injustice and the transgressions against women and children, those abused, trafficked and so on. They've become passive and unable to stand up to all the tyranny occurring in the world. They're measured instead on how much they can bench press, how many chicks they've banged and how fast or how much alcohol they can drink. Tattoos and trendy beards are masculine veneers used to cover up their feminization. Some guys even use their girlfriends as shields against aggressive men who hit on them or grab their asses. A real man would defend his woman; he wouldn't let her disrespect him by flirting with other guys in front of him. Women know these types of men don't have any balls or will do anything to defend them.

The *feminine* is rising and needs to be supported by the *masculine.* The spotlight focuses only on how the *patriarchy* is *destroying* everything and not on how women are attacked and inverted. The *feminine* is what will heal the world, NOT feminism. *Softness and grace are a woman's greatest gift; protection and service are his gifts,* and perhaps why they're heavily targeted and suppressed. The masculine and feminine are both in need of healing and restoration. We need to work through these distortions and face the shadows that are cast by these self-serving schemes. What's the cost of continuing to allow this *insanity* to happen? They want us to keep fighting and stay ignorant; we're being tricked into false subjugation. Currently, the pendulum is swinging wildly, and it will take time to balance. It's unfortunate that historically, the pendulum has never found or stayed in its centre. Maybe it's not meant to...

## WOMEN ARE SACRED

Women are sacred and their sanctity is unimpeachable. All human life passes through the *womb*man. Birth and death are the portals between one reality into another; she is the gateway into this world. She's the doorway and gatekeeper between the spiritual and physical realms; an alchemist.

Being the vessel that distils spirit into flesh and the creator of life itself, she has the power to *nurture, manipulate, or destroy.* Myths and fairy tales depict her dualistic nature. Snow White had both inner and outer beauty, in contrast, the evil witch possessed internal and external darkness. I believe if every man witnessed childbirth, women would be respected with higher regard. This is why women are targeted; they possess great influence. They are exploited by businesses, corporations and advertising agencies, this is inarguably evident. Influencing the influencers is a clever tactic, as men and children will adjust their behaviour to accommodate a woman's wants and desires.

The reverence of a woman and the mystical power of her womb is no longer considered sacred but as something threatening and needing to be controlled. She has been *objectified.*

Men may try taming her, but she cannot be; no longer burned at the stake. To feel a woman's *true magic,* one must pass through her gates of *initiation.* Men must satiate the guardians of her eyes, ears and nose. He must be pleasing to her in sight, sound, and smell. Next, he's to gratify her skin; how he touches and makes her feel will grant him passage to the next portal, her mouth. He's almost there… pleasure the rest of her body and sensitive areas until finally, he arrives and is granted access to her Holy Grail.

Bypassing or disrespecting her grace through force or lack of foreplay, he cannot experience the enchantment of her *womb.* Even sadder, is when she doesn't honour her own sanctity and authority as the guardian of her body… and lotus flower. When she betrays the keepers designed to filter out inauthentic lovers, she's doing herself a great disservice. By discounting her value and worth, she suffers. Her agency is violated and her self-respect and healthy boundaries are destroyed.

Women as mothers are the glue that holds the family together. She's the core and the heart of the menage. It's tragic for any parent to die as both are vital. However, there's something special about the *mother,* the family is hit harder when she passes. I truly felt this when my grandmother died, and later, my mother. We came from a large Italian family with a lot of cousins, aunts and uncles. Christmas and holiday gatherings were magical… until our *matriarchs* perished. The core weakened, and we began drifting away.

I remember in grade school, the girls used to be the peacekeepers outside in the schoolyard, at recess or after school. They were the moral compass, possessing care and compassion. The girls were opposed to bullying and the boys listened to them when they said to stop fighting. They stood up for what was right. Nowadays, women seem to be the instigators and align with men's immoral behaviour. They're socially programmed to benefit from the income they provide. These include violent careers and jobs which require following orders from authorities, which are sometimes unethical. Women have lost their care; they don't realize the influence they have to put an end to violence, disrespect and toxic masculinity that's rampant today.

## DESECRATION OF FEMININE

Feminism teaches men and women are equal, and that she can also sleep around. Thanks to birth control pills, media, movies, and pop culture, she's empowered and can be more selfish and sexually free. These influences promote the acceptance of casual sex. As a result, sexual standards have gone down and having sex on the first date is normalized. Maidens once were revered for a reason; free love has supplanted traditional values on sexual morality or waiting for the right person. So what's the big deal anyway?

Why do women lie about their sexual body count by lowering it, while guys embellish it? Why does society give women demerit points and guys merit points for having multiple partners? Is it the evil patriarchy, male privilege and double standards? Even women discredit other women by slut shaming them. Instinctively, they know guys prefer to settle down with those who have low body counts. Some are proud to share their high kill rate and others take it to their grave. I know women with very high numbers who have no regrets. Power to them, it's their body and their choice. Who am I to judge? I'm also sensitive to the fact that promiscuity can be the result of sexual abuse, self-esteem issues, or even depression.

When I get involved with a woman, I want to know if she is promiscuous. If she says, "My past is not your business and it has nothing to do with us," I'll tell her otherwise and the impact it may have *on us*. Wouldn't you want to know if your partner was a recovered alcoholic or drug addict? Would you be okay if they withheld that information from you? What if you found out after months of investing in them? You'd want to know if they were one drink or line away from a seven-day bender that would empty your bank account. Or end up in jail? How happy would you be to know this after you got into a serious relationship with them? This isn't about guys being insecure, it's biology. If women want to be empowered, I'm all for it, but there are factors to be considered.

There are other repercussions promiscuity can cause beyond the possibility of catching STIs. Statistically, *the more partners a woman has the less she's able to pair bond.* This also affects her ability to be *faithful*. Promiscuous women also experience higher levels of depression and an increased tenancy to abuse substances. Guys have legit concerns, they don't want to be cheated on or have to raise another man's kids. He has to trust her ability to stay faithful to ensure the baby is his. Women have been known to tie down guys who'd be better dads who aren't their kid's fathers because the real ones are trash.

In 1999 a landmark study conducted by the American Association Of Blood Banks reported that *thirty percent* of DNA paternity tests were negative. In 2019, a report by a Caribbean company offering DNA testing noted, out of all their company's paternity tests conducted since 2015, *seventy percent* of those tested were not the father. I believe paternity testing should be standard at birth.

Another study concluded, multiple sex partners before marriage reduced marital quality for women, but not for men. I don't believe guys should be whores either. Some are opportunistic dogs and don't care who they screw when they want to have fun. But *it matters* when they want to settle down and invest in a serious relationship. Ironically, women aren't as concerned about the number of partners a guy has and this may even work to his advantage; he's desired by other women; he's in de*mand*. This is why he's more concerned with her *past*, and she's more concerned with his *future* (potential). It also confirms how jealousy affects men and women differently. He doesn't want her to cuck him (to have sex with other men), and she doesn't want him to build an emotional attachment with other women, as she risks losing his resources.

## DEVALUED GOODS

Men are born from it and spend the rest of their lives trying to get back in. Women can't let every Dick, Peter and Willy in, she has to be careful and safeguard her treasure. Sadly, social pressure, media programming, and the need for validation have caused more women to leave their basement doors unlocked.

Women who give up their *goods* easily think it's what men want, but this always backfires. They won't respect her, they'll just *pump and dump.* How many other guys did she give it up to? He got his candy for free. Why should he invest? Yes, a guy also wants to feel special; he wants to know he's earned it. A guy won't claim ownership of the town bicycle. Why would he?

Everyone else has ridden on it, and he's probably had fun riding it too. If he's serious about buying a car, he'll want a new one, or at least one gently used with low mileage. If he can't afford it, he'll take what's available at the used car lot. Successful men want quality, just like women seek in them. There's a saying in the red-pilled dating community, "She's not yours, it's just your turn." If every key can open the lock, it's a shitty lock.

A toaster made in the same plant overseas will have a different perceived value depending on where and how it's sold. You can buy the same product at a discount store or a high-end boutique; a woman's *vagina is the same.* When something is abundant and easy to access, the less valuable it becomes. If everything was made from gold, it wouldn't be worth as much. These days pussy can be had instantly with a simple swipe or click of a button.

When I see women post provocative or spicy content on social media, I think, "What if they posed like that in actuality?" What's the difference between a real-life or a virtual peep show? Why's it okay for any random guy to have the ability to gawk endlessly, and possibly jerk off to her, but not okay for another to do the same if he was standing in front of her? To me, there's no difference, he's a creep and she's complying. Guys who are okay with their girlfriends running thirst trap accounts (enticing viewers sexually) on social media *are not men.* I wouldn't stand for it, "You're my woman, only I get to see you that way, no one else!" If she doesn't stop, she doesn't respect you. Men shouldn't be going after 304s (hoes) in the first place.

Ladies, you dictate the sexual economy. You can either capitalize on a guy's innate need to procreate or go on strike. You can give away your goods for free because you want his approval, or you can close your legs until he shows he's committed to you. Men are opportunists, especially if sex is offered without any strings attached.

Maybe, I'm just old fashioned at heart and believe dating today is misguided. Once upon a time, people looked for a partner to marry. They took the time to get to know a person and invest in them Today, it's like going to the clothing store and trying on all the clothes. If they don't fit, they're simply tossed into the return bin, or hung aimlessly back on the rack. I feel bad for the store clerks who have to rehang and fold them, *so they look perfect again.*

Have we become the casualties of a manipulated society? Did we lose our sovereignty and critical thinking?

# CHAPTER SEVEN

# IT'S TIME TO GROW UP

## EVOLVE OR REPEAT

Even before the world gets to us and attempts to remodel our reality, we've been forged by our parents the second air fills our tender lungs. So much can go wrong, and it usually does. *The way a twig is bent is how the tree will grow.* We've all been twisted the same way. Our early nurturing has a profound effect on our ability to bond and interact with other people; so do *traumatic events, unmet needs and disempowering beliefs.* They are the roadblocks to having healthy and happy relationships, not only with others but with ourselves. These experiences affect our identity formation, maturity level, ability to *trust* and *bond* with another. They also influence our confidence, self-esteem, and of course, our *masculine and feminine polarities.* Wouldn't it have been so much easier if we were single and unhappy simply because we are just too picky? I wish it were that way, believe me.

Beyond our physical needs, we also have emotional ones. We need more than just being fed and having our asses wiped; we need to be *seen, heard, loved, appreciated,* and given the freedom to *express ourselves.* In a perfect world, this would be par for the course. Unfortunately, it's not. What we didn't get emotionally from our parents we look to others to satiate. Unmet emotional needs create *issues* later in our adult life, and who doesn't have them? Don't we all? So what happens when we don't get what we need? An emotional deficit is created, which then needs to be addressed and resolved.

Subconsciously, we attract people with similar characteristics as our parents. This occurs so we can *replay our* repressed *wounds* and *betrayals;* so they can be healed. We attract partners who mirror our parent's shortcomings or lack of love, so we can finally prove that *we are lovable.* This continues until we finally learn the lessons. Have you noticed you attract similar types of people? Some may be a slight upgrade, but they'll usually have the same patterns, just with a different face.

An unhealthy upbringing is responsible for our lack of self-worth, fear of being smothered, abandoned, rejected and other personality disorders. *For the emotionally wounded, normal and nice is boring; the toxic bad boy or bitch is much more exhilarating.* Those who can't stimulate or play out our wounds appear invisible to us. Damaged people don't know what healthy is, even when it's staring them right in the face. *We attract those who are vibrating at our level; those who mimic our parent's failings.*

You may desire a deep connection, but you've been conditioned to feel intimacy isn't safe. So you choose unavailable partners or ones who will confirm your low self-worth. When that relationship ends, the rejection you feel reconfirms your belief *intimacy isn't safe,* and on it goes. Each toxic relationship thereafter, further adds to your confusion and reinforces the notion that *you're broken.* You're not given the opportunity to experience anything new because you're stuck in a toxic spin cycle. You'll look for others who'll fit your traumatized identity, regardless of trying to make better choices. Consciously, you want someone different, but your unconscious will betray you because it favours the familiar. *You don't have to fix others to be worthy, and you don't need to change them.* If you want to hear a different song on the radio, you'll need to change the dial; *your beliefs.* Find someone who's already gone through their shit, one who won't give you theirs.

You may believe you're free from trauma, that is until someone comes along and triggers a hidden wound. They'll push a magic button you never knew you had. Out of nowhere, you react! You do your best to avoid getting triggered, but without success. Unbeknownst to you, those wounds are navigating your life, you're on autopilot. Slowly, you find yourself enmeshed in yet another unhealthy relationship—*in a trauma bond.* You won't know why, but you will blame your partner. If you've ever experienced a traumatic event, you may become stuck emotionally at the age it happened. This prevents you from maturing any further from that point on. Some may never mature or get the chance to pass through the necessary initiations into adulthood.

## RITE OF PASSAGE

Sparta was a warrior-classed society in ancient Greece that produced strong males and very educated women. Spartan boys would be taken from their families by the age of seven, then they were trained and fortified. After a few years, usually by age ten, they were sent off alone into the wilderness with only a spear and a blanket. If they came back after a month, it would mean they had succeeded. If any returned within one to two weeks, or if at all… they failed. When the boys completed their training, they would become official Spartans, celebrated and given a wife. Spartan females were taught many things, including, gymnastics, culture, music and even some light combat. If she excelled between the ages of eighteen and twenty, she'd be assigned a husband. Spartan women had more status and freedom than other Greek women.

Some religious organizations still recognize these rites of passage. Whether it's a *Confirmation* observed by the Catholic Church, a *Baptism* in an evangelical congregation, or the celebration of the *Bar Mitzvah* in the Jewish faith, young boys and girls partake in similar ceremonies. Indigenous cultures and tribes around the world also practice these rites. All share three phases, *separation, transition, and re-incorporation.* They are found in every myth and legend. The hero *leaves*—the hero *struggles*—and the hero comes back *transformed.* These phases are also utilized by the military.

Young men are taken from home and sent away to be enlisted, their heads are shaved and they're given a uniform; to detach them from their former identity. Then they're taught new skills and put through rigorous training; they're yelled at and broken down—to *get seasoned.* When they pass these tests, they graduate and are re-introduced into their community. Whichever tribe or group oversees these types of rituals, there's always a celebration and feast observed in conclusion. This is done to recognize the initiate's transition into manhood, new status and privilege.

So why the history lesson? Adults today are *underdeveloped children stuck in older bodies.* Boys are no longer initiated into the rituals of *separation, initiation,* and the *return* process. The family unit has become unstable or has been destroyed. Old wisdom is lost and thus cannot be passed down the generational line. The container required for proper initiation is no longer available and the challenges in need of conquering are absent. They're substituted with overprotection, coddling and helicopter parenting. Manhood has been replaced with Peter Pans and snowflakes, boys who still want mommy to be their girlfriend. Sadly, boys haven't weaned off their superheroes; their focus only changes from caped heroes to those wearing helmets who score goals. Boys need strong role models and unfortunately, there aren't many true heroes left to mentor them.

How can males become leaders when they're still in mommy's basement playing video games and getting high? Actors, athletes and gaming have become surrogates; they battle against fabricated challenges and obstacles, which have been designed to satiate man's innate drive to lead and conquer.

## EMOTIONAL MATURITY

Do you ever wonder why your woman acts like a whiny or bossy little girl? Does your guy act like a clueless man-child, one you have to take care of? Has sex become flat, a chore, or unenjoyable? The majority of current relationships are *underdeveloped* and *unbalanced.* Healthy relationships are composed of two adults who interact respectfully with one another.

Unfortunately, this isn't the case for most. Typical relationships involve a parent/child, or a child/child dynamic. This means one person acts as a parent and the other like a child. The most detrimental relationship occurs when both act like children *but pretend to be adults.* Imagine two six-year-olds playing house together. These two imbalances lead to codependent and depolarized relationships. *There's no sexual attraction between a parent and child, mother and son, or father and daughter.* Partners in a healthy relationship are treated equally.

Adulthood demands we leave the nest and return when we're ready. The three phases in the *rites of passage* also apply to healthy parental disengagement: *attachment, detachment and integration.* In other words, mutual *dependence, struggle,* and *interdependence.* As children, we have no sense of *boundaries*; when we become adults and learn this periphery, we're better able to honour them. Our parents become our *advisers* or *mentors.* Unfortunately, some remain as our *tormentors.*

The Intelligence Quotient or IQ is the measure of how smart someone is. Emotional Intelligence (EQ) is an individual's ability to identify, evaluate, control and express *emotions.* People with high EQ or *emotional maturity* can identify and manage emotions calmly and respectfully; they have compassion and understanding toward another's feelings. Those with low EQ are usually confrontational, quick to anger, selfish and don't have any regard for another's feelings or perspectives. They're typically childish and impulsive; they don't consider the potential consequences of their actions.

You've either emotionally matured, or you haven't. There is no faking it because eventually, it always surfaces. Look at how children fight over a toy and name-call. "You hit me first!" "No, you did!" It's back and forth blaming, criticizing and giving each other the silent treatment. Neither one wants to take any responsibility. Adults can address and resolve conflicts as they arise; children have a harder time doing that. *Grown-ups* take responsibility for their actions and know how to communicate without blaming anyone. Mature adults take others' feelings into account; they aren't selfish and can see the bigger picture— they've developed *compassion.* They want to understand and communicate without using manipulation or engaging in power struggles; there's mutual respect for one another. Only selfishly absorbed children attack and throw tantrums when they don't get their way; they kick and scream until they get what they want. How many couples do you know who fight like this?

## YES MOMMY

With the rise of single mothers and absentee fathers, *children are suffering.* Even in stable, two-parent families, the young can fall victim to *distorted programming.* For instance, mothers typically make the mistake of teaching their sons how to treat women. If this triggers you and makes you want to attack me, it may be a part of the reason why toxic masculinity isn't properly addressed. We've heard it before, *"Treat her nice and be a gentleman,"* and that's the problem. She's setting him up to fail. Why? Since there's no sexual attraction between a mother and her son *(we only hope),* she's showing him how to be a woman's best friend and a boring platonic nice guy. Nevertheless, mothers must teach their sons how to *honour* and *respect* women; therein lies the difference.

A mother will always love her son more than she does his father; this love is distinct and unconditional. Men receive a different type of affection from their mothers than they do from their lovers. Guys need to grasp this and stop excepting *mommy love* from their women. *And if you're over eighteen, it's time to do your own fucking laundry.* Guys, you've been duped by fairy tales and social programming. Perverted fetishes aside, if your woman loves you like a son, *you've got problems.* This is why a *son's boyhood love* for his mother has to die for him to become a man. He has to cut the umbilical cord and get off her tit, or forever be a *mamma's boy.* Instinctively, he knows this, and it shows through his attempts at playing loud music, leaving a messy room and resisting doing chores. Hence, the Irish saying, "A son is a son till he takes him a wife, a daughter is a daughter all of her life".

I'm not saying to disrespect your mother; *honour her* but stop trying to *please her.* You can see this unhealthy dynamic in grown men, especially from single mothers'. "My mama this, and my mama that." Unfortunately, the feminine is also wounded. Women remain little girls with closed hearts they need to protect. This is a topic that deserves more attention, perhaps in another book or course.

Mothers play a different role for their daughters; they initiate them into womanhood. She helps shave her legs, buys her first bra, accompanies her to get her ears pierced, helps with applying makeup, tampons or pads, etc. I respect single dads who can help their daughters through these rites of passage alone. Dads also have to detach from their daughters and accept when they grow into womanhood.

## WHERE IS DADDY?

"Your daddy is an asshole, and we don't need him." said the woman who blames the guy *she chose* to be her baby daddy. He may very well have been a lying narcissist, but that's a discussion for another time. Yes, *anyone can be a father, but it takes a man to become a dad.*

Children need both their mom and dad to receive balanced parenting; *it's a team effort.* Their roles thrive for different reasons and at different stages in a child's life. Mothers offer *nourishment,* and fathers provide *discipline.* Fathers teach their sons what their mothers cannot, and vice versa. Fathers don't hold the container for the separation experience; *detaching from mom.* He can only *show them the exit* from her. He's there to facilitate the initiation—*the night in the wild*—so he can return later as a man. What happens when dad's not around? Single moms are *forced to turn masculine* to compensate for the absence of dad's influence and leadership. This is causing significant problems.

Toxic masculinity isn't the issue; young men today no longer have healthy role models. Did you know to date, about *forty-three percent* of boys are being raised by single mothers, and *seventy-eight percent* of teachers are women? Evidence shows fatherless males haven't been taught strong boundaries, limits, discipline, or how to manage their anger. Statistics show that male children of single mothers have a greater risk of suffering poverty, behavioural problems, suicide, substance abuse, imprisonment, and dropping out of school. Boys need their mothers for their early nurturing, then later, their fathers for self-control and regulation. Boys not only need to detach from mommy but from daddy too. They need to do so without vilifying him.

Dads have a huge responsibility not only for their sons but for their daughters. If daddy messes up, he can severely destroy her self-esteem and body image. Mom can compliment all she wants, but it will fall on deaf ears. When dad speaks, it drills through instantly. A daughter's confidence is a direct response to what her daddy thinks of her. Girls without a father are *three times* more likely to get pregnant before they're eighteen. Dads are always on them for not dressing slutty and are constantly giving her warnings of what some guy's intentions are. This may not stop her totally from being irresponsible or promiscuous, but it helps her become aware and possibly help regulate that behaviour.

The time eventually comes when a father hears those dreaded words from his wife, "Honey, Jenny got her period today." He has to concede his sweet daughter is now a woman and no longer his innocent little girl. Suddenly he has a new interest in polishing guns over his lap as he interrogates his daughter's male friends when they come over to visit.

## MARRYING OUR PARENTS

I remember when my sister first introduced her *"boyfriend"* to the family. She dated guys before, but this was the first one she showcased. She said, "OMG, he has the same birthday as daddy." I said, "So it's true, *we do* marry our parents." She was surprised I made such a bold prediction about her future husband. Typically in Italian culture, we only bring home marriage material. I did the same, nobody knew who I dated before I brought home the woman who was going to be my wife.

Our parents have a direct bearing on our self-esteem and bonding style. If you didn't feel safe expressing your emotions, you won't later with your partner. If mom was domineering, then you're more prone to attract a similar type of woman. Attracting emotionally unavailable men could be because dad left the family when you were young. Your distorted view of the masculine can be the result of having a father who couldn't stand up or protect you from a controlling mother. Maybe you've learned femininity is a weakness because mom didn't protect you from dad's angry outbursts, and vice versa. Some guys had toxic fathers, which they would emulate or vow never to become like. They'd either become the same asshole or cut their balls off to prove they weren't like him. Overly dominant mothers could have a similar effect on their daughters. If daddy didn't have any balls, then Susy would grow a set of her own.

If either of your parents were: emotionally or physically abusive or absent, a narcissist, an addict, over critical or controlling, unfaithful, had unclear boundaries, lacked communication skills, had unrealistic expectations, stopped you from expressing your opinions and emotions, compared you to other kids, blamed or projected onto you, lacked responsibility, used you for emotional support, and/or didn't afford you your independence; you've probably experienced some form of unhealthy relationship; romantically or otherwise. In my case, I had a domineering mother who I would placate for approval. This later extended to my future partners. I was emasculated, depolarized and inverted. As result, I became passive and approval-seeking.

The way to a healthy and stable relationship is by growing up and becoming an adult—by detaching from any parental co-dependencies, by healing and releasing all the emotional relics from your childhood. *You're not yet fully an adult if you're still emotionally triggered by either of your parents.*

We need to become our own person and separate from our parents. Only then can we be an adult in our relationships.

# CHAPTER EIGHT

# MEN & WOMEN ARE NOT CREATED EQUAL

## EQUALLY DISTINCT

Now before you attempt to lynch me and chase me with torches, hear me out. Men and women are not the same, but *they're equally important*. Both have been created to balance each other; offering opposite traits that *aren't integrated within themselves*. Each possesses different strengths. *Not being equal* doesn't mean a man is superior to a woman; I'd say quite the contrary. Equality doesn't equal sameness. I may not agree with antiquated advertisements portraying women as slaves who only cooked and cleaned, but I do regarding women as having greater emotional and intuitive strength. Those ads were preposterous and sexist, they'd never fly today, but they were depictions of that era. I believe we've come a long way since then. Our differences are not being honoured; this is killing our attraction to each other.

## WE'RE STILL NEANDERTHALS

Whether we're a product of an incestuous biblical story, have evolved from primates or have been seeded here by aliens, our species is biologically hardwired to *survive and replicate*. Our primary purpose is survival and our second is to reproduce. After they are addressed, we can pursue intellectual and spiritual fulfillment; if one chooses to evolve that is. Regardless of all the technological advancements we have today and the rise of women's empowerment movements, our DNA and primal impulses are still paramount. Men don't bonk women over the head anymore. *The conditions may have changed, but our wiring has not.* Men need women to reproduce and pass down their genes; women need their protection and provision for survival. Modern advancements are making our lives easier, but also more confusing. Women can now be the hunters and men the gatherers.

A guy is programmed to spread his seed to as many females as possible. He has to learn to override this urge if he's in a monogamous relationship, especially if he doesn't want to be paying out his ass in child support payments. I'm sure if untethered, he'd procure a harem and act more like a bull or rooster. Males produce about eight billion sperm in one full regenerative cycle *(sixty-four days)*. Since each load of ejaculate contains *twenty to one hundred million* sperm, he would only need about *eighty* orgasms to populate the entire Earth.

Females are born with around one million eggs that they inherit from their mothers. This means mom's babies are a combination of her lover's sperm and the ovum granny produced. Hmm... This is why genes are believed to skip a generation.

Women don't produce eggs as hens do; they're given only a finite bag of marbles. By the time puberty hits, a female will only have around *three hundred thousand* eggs left. Out of those, only *three hundred* are available for ovulation during her reproductive lifetime. Over *ninety percent* of her eggs are gone by *thirty.*

Every *twenty-eight days,* one (or more) of her eggs drop and are ready for fertilization. She has only so many eggs in her life to bear children and that is why she has to be *very selective* about who she shares them with. *She can't wait too long.* Guys have a longer mating window and can father children much later in life by comparison. A woman's mating cycle is only *once per month and a man's is once a day.* Both egg and sperm quality decrease with age.

Physically, pregnant women are vulnerable, their bodies also change during and after childbirth. As a result, her SMV may be lower, which can be a disadvantage if she were to enter the single market again. There's more at stake for her, she has to know her guy is all in. She needs him to remain monogamous, as it would be bad for business if his resources were divided elsewhere. Mom needs the safety and provision a dad can provide to better her and their baby's odds of survival. He can bounce at any time and leave her holding the stork bag. Financial obligations need to be considered as well, as raising a kid costs the same as buying a Lamborghini.

Men have the advantage of strength, which women need to leverage, so they can benefit from it. This is why she desires the strongest and healthiest male in the tribe. She can fend for herself if he's not around; as mama bears can become quite vicious if their babies are ever threatened. In tribes, women most often choose the man returning with the fresh kill draped over his shoulders and not the one who is following behind holding his spear. Similarly, men will choose women who are gentle, radiant and nurturing over the frigid-insensitive-bitch-faced-ball-breakers. He will also choose the healthiest and most beautiful woman available to better ensure his chances of fathering genetically superior children. *Genetics is dictating, "Why would a guy want to spread his seed to a woman who is resistant to him? Similarly, why would a woman submit to a beta male who isn't able to protect and provide?"*

## EMOTIONAL VS SEXUAL INTIMACY

Emotional intimacy for men is considered a risk. Boys are taught not to cry; they learn how to repress their emotions. If men show they're vulnerable, they're deemed *weak*, or toxic if they express stronger feelings, like aggression. Women are *expected* to feel and express themselves emotionally, so emotional intimacy isn't as perilous. The reverse applies to sexual intimacy; for men, having sex isn't a risk, but for women it is—they can get knocked up. Granted, better education and birth control methods are affording women more control over their decision to bear children. Men are praised for having multiple partners and are called *studs*. Women with the same appetite are labelled *whores*.

Women need emotional intimacy to have sex and men need sex to feel it. *This creates conflict.* Women complain men can't understand their emotional needs; he interprets this as drama, bitching, nagging and complaining. For her, they aren't theatrics, they're her emotional frustrations of not being *heard* and *understood*. She'll shut off when she feels no connection, which means no sex for him. Men see this as rejection and not being loved, to him getting sex means *acceptance* and emotional *connection*. Her ability to open up *sexually* is proportional to his willingness to open up *emotionally*. Are guys too emotionally shut off and unable to empathize? Is this why they have a harder time *understanding* women? Is this why heterosexual women have the least amount of sexual enjoyment and experience fewer orgasms than straight males, gays and lesbians?

Men fall in love with what they see and women fall for what they hear. Is this why women wear makeup and guys will say anything to get in their pants? Men's sexual desire is activated mainly by visual cues; *he's aroused by desire.* Although she can also become aroused visually, women become fully aroused by *being desired.* They need more cues; a combination of visual and psychological. These include romance, confidence, personality, words, touch, scent, etc. Men typically enjoy porn as it's more visual, while women respond better to Literotica, fantasy and the spoken word. My advice to men; *it's all about how you make her feel.* If she feels *cherished and desired,* she's yours. Women need to feel *appreciated* and may cheat if they aren't.

During sexual arousal, stimulation and penetration, women release *oxytocin,* a bonding hormone; *more so after an orgasm.* Men have a better ability *to detach* and don't get as attached after sex. Our Creator made it this way. The bonding hormone oxytocin doesn't lend itself well to hunting and killing, as it lowers his *testosterone.* The tribe wouldn't survive if men formed bonds with their prey. Vegetarian is an old Indigenous word for, *bad hunter.* Since women are more emotional, their behaviour can become more intense and sometimes seem erratic when she's upset. If she goes postal on you, it means she's invested and has feelings for you. She won't get to that point if you are leading and devoted to her.

Some women have learned to disconnect like males can, however, it's much harder for them to do so. Especially if they're *empathic and emotional.* Factors that can help her unhook are alcohol, drugs, anger, revenge, past trauma, or simply boredom. Some women are left-brain dominant and possess less empathy than those ruled by their right brain; they can detach easier. Women seek an *emotional connection,* which is rare to receive from most men; this is why they *value* it so much.

## MAN VERSUS WOMAN

We have to stop competing and trying to prove which sex is superior. There will never be a head-to-head winner because we're different. Victory will be achieved when we begin to understand our differences. As mentioned on the back cover of this book, you can't pound a square peg into a round hole. Guys *rationalize* more and use less emotion; although women also use logic, they're more *empathic* and relate to their *feelings.*

The human brain is divided into two halves, the *left* and the *right.* The right side is responsible for *feelings,* the left is for *logic.* They are held together by a thick band of fibres called the *corpus callosum.* This allows both sides of the brain to communicate via chemical and electrical signals. A woman's corpus callosum is thicker and can better access both hemispheres, and this is why women are considered to be more complex, even without factoring in hormones.

I once heard a comedian say, "A man's brain is more compartmentalized, like a stack of boxes—a woman's brain is more like a ball of yarn. Men need to open and close each box one at a time, whereas her entangled string connects everything." Men have an on-and-off switch, and women have a complex motherboard full of faders, dials and buttons. A woman once said, "Women can multitask, but guys can't." If this were true, why can't women have sex and a headache at the same time?

Women retain stronger memories of emotional events than men. This is why they accuse guys of not caring, but they do. Men are also less affected by the chemical soup of hormones women experience. This can drastically affect her body and moods; even food can alter her blood sugar levels. Also, men don't experience monthly menses or menopause. It's almost as if women *want* men to be more *complicated. What he says, means what he says.* Ladies, stop reading more into it—*this drives a guy nuts.* I know you want him to understand and experience life as you do, but he can't. Men's brains work differently no matter how much you want it otherwise. Although our differences do cause conflicts, they're essential and provide *balance.* They offer different points of view so that we can navigate through life better, *together.*

Women say, "*I love you*" more often, but men say "I love you" first, *sixty-one percent* of the time. Believe it or not, guys are more romantic and catch feelings sooner. According to a 2013 survey conducted by eHarmony, men take an average of *three months* to tell a woman he loves her. Whereas, women do so at around *four and a half months.* Guys seem to believe women love them the same way they do—*they don't.* Men's propensity to romance can lead them to believe in love at first sight, but due to her biology and its risks, she's more pragmatic about it. Love for her needs to develop slowly; she needs to be sure he's her best option. Jumping in too fast can lead to more than just *nine months* of holding the stork bag.

Women sometimes challenge me and say *men don't commit.* They do... but, they have a reason for getting cold feet. Men are not afraid of *commitment;* they're afraid of *entrapment.* They want to commit, but only if they feel free to do so—*it needs to be their choice.* Entering a committed relationship involves sacrificing parts of ourselves. A man gives up his agency to have multiple partners as his instincts prompt him—women surrender their natural tendency to usurp and control. Why do you think *porn and feminism* are so popular? They pander to these instincts.

A man's nature is to fix, create and devote to things he cherishes. This is why he takes pride and joy in working on his car. He'll commit to protecting and beautifying her, hence why cars are called *she.* He's self-motivated through his autonomy and not because he's forced to. I'm sure he wouldn't commit to his car if *she* was able to complain or talk back.

Men and women demonstrate aggression differently. He shows it *physically* and she does *psychologically.* Guys get angry and will use *force* and women retaliate by utilizing *degradation.* She will *shame, guilt and insult* one's character. Since men know their physical strength can be destructive, they'll need to practice self-constraint. Men generally shut off emotionally and don't talk as much so they don't provoke violence, or appear too vulnerable.

Although women are not as strong as men, they are by and large *emotionally and psychologically* superior. They need to be more intuitive, especially as mothers. How else can they anticipate their baby's needs when crying is their only form of communication? She's developed the empathy to feel others' emotional states much better than men. In some cases, *she feels* another's emotions as if they were her own. In contrast, men are less empathic and are geared more towards *solutions and fixing problems.*

Women flourish by being *cherished and supported* by men and by the support and *interconnectedness* of other women. Guys thrive by being *admired and inspired* by women and through the *critique and competition* from other men.

## THERE ARE ONLY TWO GENDERS

I firmly believe that *biologically,* there are only two genders, with an exception. Biochemically, a fetus is born with either XY or XX chromosomes. They have a *penis or vagina*; males produce *sperm*—females provide *eggs.* Genitals have evolved for one another; they fit. Sperm fertilizes the ova like pollen pollinates the ovules of a flower; like *stamens and pistils.* Bulls don't produce milk and roosters don't lay eggs, etc. There is however a 0.05% chance of having both sets of chromosomes at conception, *which produces both genitalia.* These individuals are called, hermaphrodites, or Intersex people.

Gender confusion occurs when a person *chooses to identify* with one or more of the many categories of gender identity. These are *mental, emotional* and perhaps *spiritual* paradigms, they're not physical. *Male and female* are terms used to describe the biological sex or gender of a human or non-human animal and organisms. *Masculine and feminine* are idioms used when describing *gender traits* or their *characteristics.* Our Soul, in its purest state, is *genderless*. Technically, you can identify as a male or a female in whatever body you're assigned with. No one should be denied this choice. However, one's DNA is what it is; it's their biological blueprint.

You may modify or remove pieces by surgery or hormones, but as successful as this may be on the surface, one can never fully replace the skeletal system and muscles of the other gender. They can only attempt to *override* the hormonal neurotransmitters *naturally produced* from their DNA. A man identifying as a woman will never truly know a menstrual cycle or experience the labour pain a biological woman undergoes. These and other initiations *into womanhood,* are completely bypassed.

You can modify the body of a compact vehicle into a race car in the same way. It may look like a fast car, but it will never perform like one. Moreover, if the driver of that car believes to be a competitive racer and handles it as such, it will overheat and break down quickly. The car wasn't designed for that amount of load to be placed on it. What would happen if the same driver tried racing a tractor-trailer? Now, if they drove a supercar specifically made for handling hairpin turns at high speeds; the car would thrive in those conditions. There would considerably, be less wear and tear on the vehicle and greater satisfaction for the driver. Your body, which is your assigned sex, *is the car,* and you are the driver.

You can identify as either Michael or Michelle Schumacher, but you're still at the mercy of the car you're driving. Unfortunately, we've developed to a point in our society where *feelings* are more important than *scientific facts.* Stating these facts or disagreeing with inverted narratives will get you caught in the net of wokeness. Hurt feelings are being used as weapons to shame and blackmail those challenging or in disagreement with this nonsense. I've been called a genderphobe, an anti-this and a pro-that, as a result. I'm far from any of these degrading labels, and if you must, reread pages *v* and *vi*. You may feel upset at this reality, but biology wins every time.

## MR. MOM & MRS. DAD

Men and women *can* reverse roles, both in the workplace and in domestic relationships. They *can* even do it *better* than the other. If this dynamic works for you, then who am I to disagree? The changing dynamics of social and economic norms are forcing many of us to adapt. More men are staying home as caregivers cooking and cleaning, while women are out being the breadwinners. Jobs and domestic duties are becoming less identified by gender specificity. Women are more financially independent and no longer need a guy's income. She doesn't even need his penis—science is ready to give her a baby. Dating and marriage are now voluntary and no longer a *necessity*. This affords women more discretion and the opportunity to choose a higher-value guy.

This role reversal creates lots of confusion in men; they don't know their place or how to behave anymore. Many have given up and have stopped pursuing women or relationships altogether. Many men have lost their sense of purpose; they've also lost all they've worked hard for through *infidelity and divorce.* Many no longer have the drive to *provide or succeed* in life. Some have even eschewed luxury and have chosen instead, to live simply and well within their means.

Optically, the amalgamation of gender roles is a win for equality, but sooner or later, biology kicks in and starts causing havoc. Men and women have different hormonal makeups, which affect each body differently. Men function better with more *testosterone* present and women do better with higher levels of *estrogen and oxytocin.* When these are inverted it causes stress, and both suffer. As testosterone increases in women due to elevated masculine behaviour, stress levels increase and estrogen decreases. Similarly, when men behave more femininely, their testosterone decreases and stress levels increase so does estrogen. It's only a matter of time before *depression and disease* arise. Medication, wine, antidepressants and unhealthy coping mechanisms are used to alleviate these imbalances. *Biologically we are different;* these biologies affect how we think and feel.

I've spoken to countless women and single mothers who've been forced into being masculine. They do everything and have to make all the decisions, it's not always because they want to, but because they feel they have no other choice. Almost all have confessed it makes them feel sick, tired and depressed. *Stress is a silent killer.*

Men are dropping the ball and women are too afraid to pass it back; *they've picked it up.* The chicken or the egg, whose fault is it? We need to play to our abilities, not against them; or we'll burn out like the car example in the last section. You can invert roles and it may work for a time, but sooner or later, nature kicks in and puts a stop to it. If you can defy biology with no ill effects, I tip my hat to you… but I wouldn't bet on it.

## REAL FEMINISM

I've never liked labels, but if I had to align with one that empowers women, I'd say I'm an ally of *classic feminism*. I support equal rights, opportunity and pay. Women should also have the freedom to wear whatever they want; *inclusivity*. What I don't support are movements like Neo feminism and male-bashing agendas that attack and divide our sexes—those who demand *additional rights* over men. Both Patri*archy* and Matri*archy* share the word *archy,* which means, *denoting a type of rule or government.* Last time I checked, *equality* means *no one rules over anyone.* Equity doesn't attack men or the patriarchy, nor subjugate females or the matriarchy.

I also challenge when gender and ethnic politics interfere with the job hiring process. Having to fill quotas based on political correctness instead of one's ability creates more problems than solutions. If one can do the job regardless of gender and skin colour, I'll hire them. If my team ends up represented by a minority or a majority group, then so be it. If two applicants are vying for the same job and one isn't physically strong enough to perform it or puts another's safety in danger, they won't get hired. Applying for a job you can't do *to prove a point* or for a political reason, is wrong and dangerous.

Over a haircut, a client and captain of the nearby Firehall told me, "I have to hire a pregnant woman of a minority over a qualified male because it would be viewed as *discrimination.*" He may have been just joking, but appeared frustrated with the whole process. Welcome to cancel culture and being held hostage for believing in common sense.

I understand the pendulum needs to swing more to one side to initiate change, but this only creates more *tension,* for it will swing back harder the other way. Sadly, women weren't allowed to enter the workforce; however, due to world wars, empowerment movements and the 19th amendment (the right for women to vote), things have changed for what I believe is for the better. *But when will it be enough?* Until men have been fully decimated and the patriarchy is dead? Is the goal to coronate the matriarchy into becoming the rulers of society just like the Nubians, Kush, Sudan Queens, Trobrianders of Papua New Guinea, Palawan of the Philippines, Khasi of India and the Mosuo of Tibet/China were? What happened to *men building the house* and *women making it a home?* We need each other's gifts; *not suppress them.*

## WORK/PAY EQUALITY

There's a common misconception surrounding pay equality. The pay gap affects *mothers and fathers* more than it does between men and women. Protesters claim men make more annually than women, but they don't base this on the actual hours worked. According to the U.S. census, the data says men work 41.0 *hours* and women do 36.3 *hours per week.* Discrepancies in pay inequality should be debated objectively, honestly and with every factor affecting it. Doing so without gender bashing, or accusations of male privilege. I support women *choosing* whatever job they want and being paid *equally* for it. I'm sure many other guys feel the same. Not all men conspire to keep women down, as some have you believe. Furthermore, The Equal Pay Act of 1963 says sex-based pay discrimination is illegal. Does it still happen? Maybe.

Historically, this imbalance was born out of *necessity, circumstance and biology.* As new paradigms unfold, older archetypes get challenged. This is what's causing the resistance between the genders; so is *misinformation.* Why is the patriarchy blamed, and every man made accountable? Our society isn't male-dominated; it's only a tiny portion of super-successful men that are used to represent this claim. It was men who went to war, who died and never came back. Guys were more willing to work longer hours and in more dangerous situations and subsequently had higher job-related deaths. They fell off the steel beams building skyscrapers and got electrocuted while attaching high voltage power lines.

Men sacrificed their lives for the comforts we all enjoy today. We have become shamed as adults for opening up about our feelings and mental states. Men can't appear weak because they might lose their job, get taken advantage of and so on. Most are afraid to get help and express their problems, so they suck it up and keep it inside. This is why men succumb to addictions, depression, and fall victim to suicide. Men self-murder *three times* more than women.

Interestingly, women who once outlived men are now dying sooner as they're experiencing similar stress and related dangers of doing *men's jobs.* Higher-paying careers usually require one to be *ruthless, have less empathy and compassion,* and an unhealthy drive to succeed. Men tend to display these characteristics more than women. Left-brained sociopaths have no problem firing workers with dependent families who could all end up living on the street. Women have more *care* and *empathy,* it's harder for them to be tyrants.

If you're a woman who doesn't want kids, has learned to throttle your empathy and is prepared to work longer hours, *then go for it.* There's no reason why you can't earn more than men. Understand, however, there's more at stake and a greater price to pay; there's a sacrifice to your *health, body and mind.* By having a more complex chemical makeup, you're more prone to hormonal fluctuations than men are. You always need to be on, emotional and physical consistency will be harder to maintain. If you do have children, you'll have to make significant concessions.

Is work more important than being available, present and active with your family? Can you hire a live-in nanny who cooks and cleans while you're working long hours? I believe all the money in the world can't replace a child's need for their mother's love and nurturing care. *Only a mother can make a house a home.* Women have a more diverse work-to-life balance than men do; being a *career woman-wife-mom* demands a double and sometimes triple workload. This almost always leads to further resentment against men. All this stress on a woman's biology leaves her feeling sick, frustrated and tired. This often causes her to leave for a *less demanding,* thus a *lower-paying* job.

Equal opportunity doesn't mean equal outcome, there are physical limitations. We talk about equality in the ceiling jobs like CEOs, lawyers and physicians, but why is there disparity with the basement jobs? You don't see many women choosing the three D's; the *dirty, dangerous and demeaning;* jobs like the trades, garbage pick up and ditch digging. Men are also more *disagreeable* and will fight for higher pay; some will even demand it. Women are more *agreeable* and tend to avoid the conflict of asking for a raise. They typically choose public sector jobs such as nursing, caregiving, physical therapy and so on. Men gravitate more to the STEM jobs like Science, Technology, Engineering and Mathematics. The more men and women are free to choose, the more different they choose to be. If women get paid less, then why wouldn't companies higher more of them to make higher profits?

Gender tendencies suggest women are more interested in *people* and men are more interested in *things*. This explains the congruency in the careers both choose and study. There's more profit to be made from creating and selling things than there is from investing in people. Caring for others means trading your *time* for money, although it offers a *greater reward, it's less pay.*

Scandinavia has the greatest workplace equality, yet they experience something called the Nordic paradox. There's still disparity and gender bias in the workplace. Although Norway has the highest workplace equality, it also has one of the world's highest divorce rates. Conversely, as of 2018, Guatemala has one of the lowest divorce rates and follows more traditional gender roles. Are the old-fashioned ways the secret to a lasting marriage?

I believe in equal pay—for equal work—for equal outcome. I don't begrudge women for wanting identical conditions in the workplace, but is this *killing attraction* and keeping us *single*? Time will tell where this is all going... and if we're on the right track.

# CHAPTER NINE

# UNDERSTANDING HER

## SECRETS WOMEN DON'T WANT MEN TO KNOW

The following two chapters focus on women and their behaviour. I could be wrong and full of shit, or maybe I'm beginning to understand women more... if that's even possible. *I'm a guy, so what do I know?* Nonetheless, it's my duty to help my fellow brethren with what I've learned. If you're a woman reading, hopefully, this can act as a mirror to help you better *innerstand* yourself. Understanding each other is the first step to happy and sustained coupling. Most guys are clueless when it comes to women. Let's open up this can of worms and see how it goes.

There are secrets women won't ever admit to, but wish men knew... but really didn't. Sound confusing? Men are to understand *her nature, not her moods.* Any attempt at trying to understand her fluctuating emotions will feminize him. Feminine energy flows with the spirit of life—unchanging yet never the same—like the *weather* and the *waves* in the ocean. Sometimes she's calm, chaotic, gentle, dark, joyful... then melancholy. She's mysterious, complex and simple. She can be accessible, then slip away into the depths of her being; inaccessible and beyond reach. Most men think they know their women until the labyrinth of their moods sinks them deep into their waters. *Don't try to understand her; you need only to lead her out of the storm.*

There's a saying, "There are no good girls, the bad ones only got caught." She's done some crazy shit on trips, behind the scenes and some you'll never know about—secrets reserved only for a few of her trusted friends.

Guys, you better sit down for this one. You're probably not her first choice. She may still be pining over the one who got away—the one who broke her heart—the guy who set the standard... *you'll never live up to.* She's haunted by him, her mind often roams and she becomes aroused by seductive images and feelings of sexual passion. You're a good man and provider, nonetheless, *she has settled for you.*

She's never alone, even if she's single. There are always men in her life in some way or another. If you're with her *exclusively,* the odds are, you've probably poached her from one or more men. Women will monkey branch, they'll set up a new relationship before pulling the plug on the current one. Sometimes, she jumps to a new one immediately after a breakup or has been in one for months. She always has a plan B, this is her insurance policy. Even if you're married and have a joint bank account, she'll most likely have a secret kitty at the ready, just in case things go south between you.

She may be spinning a few plates (keeping a rotation) when dating until she settles. I'm not saying guys don't monkey branch, they do but to a lesser extent and typically wait longer between relationships, sometimes weeks if not months. Chads and emotionally devoid men are the exceptions. When a relationship peters out or normalizes, women tend to notice it first. They'll also get bored faster and lose their desire much quicker. Guys are oblivious and will accept things as they are. She's more prone to cheat during ovulation than during her menses. Yes, women love sex; their sexual appetite and capacity can far exceed that of men. But... she doesn't want to be slut shamed, so she may act prudish or keep it secret until she's in the bedroom.

## SEXUAL FANTASIES

Why do so many romance novels involve some kind of consensual rape or assault? Do you know *thirty percent* of porn watchers are female? According to analytics monitored by a popular porn site, that number is *increasing yearly.* You'd be surprised knowing their top searches involved violent and male-dominant scenarios. Although, *lesbian* is the most searched worldwide, collectively, threesomes, hardcore, double penetration, anal and gang bang were the highest. What happened to respect *equality, feminism and sensitivity?* I believe women secretly crave being sexually dominated. In my chair, women have confessed to having secret fantasies of being raped, consensually, of course. This seems like the antithesis of what they preach, doesn't it? Women will deny this at first, but deep down in their psyche... they want to be dominated.

You have to respect a woman's need for plausible deniability. She may be bluffing and acting as if she's not crazy about sex; she just doesn't want to be *judged for being a slut.* In some cases, *she won't be pretending* and may have severe trauma due to past experiences. You need to be aware and have compassion in these situations. Never assume or push! There's a difference between *don't... stop,* and *don't stop.* Know the difference, and you can't blame it on bad grammar. If you're unsure, *No always means NO!* If you want to explore her deepest yearnings, you must build categorical trust beforehand.

Sexual fantasies are a woman's *cry of frustration* and arise from her sexual loneliness or her need for more *real sex.* Even sexually active women imagine having more sex. Why? Most are never sexually satisfied beyond their fantasies. What they don't get enough of in real life can be explored in her imagination. Furthermore, sexual desires suppressed by shame and guilt may need to be played out, especially the repressed sexual impulses had as a young girl. I've wanted to be *the guy* who makes a woman's fantasies real for her in this reality. Some are meant to be shared, while others *are not... ever.* Respect this, it's her safe place; where *no man* is permitted. Having said that, I won't stop trying to rouse them.

Few men understand the *depth of her desire,* they're unable to fathom what she's capable of conjuring up. She wants you to free her and unleash the unbridled passion from the shackles of her repressed guilt and shame. She may feel *humiliated* for having such thoughts, or she simply doesn't trust you enough to share them—let alone explore them. When you've earned her total trust, you can virtually do whatever you want to her. She'll become your insatiable whore. The reason she doesn't live out her fantasies like the novels, is because she can't imagine any man being able to let her do so in a safe way. She craves an experience of *consensual non-consent.* She wants you to *eat her heart and fuck her soul*, but she has to have *full control to reject* anything that may jeopardize her safety; *just like in her fantasies.*

"My girl is different and she wouldn't do those things." Riiight... you have no idea my friend. The things she yearns for will leave you speechless and shocked beyond belief. A wise man will know, what she does and says are two different things. A woman can't betray her nature, watch her actions, don't listen to her words. Lesser men suffer from the Madonna-whore dichotomy; if she isn't a virtuous woman, she must be a desire-driven slut who lacks morality. Newsflash, she's both your wallflower and whore, a lady in the streets and a freak in the sheets.

Guys, stop partitioning her nature... only a masculine man can elicit and handle both aspects. She wants you to step it up and coax the *savage* out of her. You'll need patience, time and absolute masculine traits to achieve this. Unfortunately, many men fail, and her only option is to escape into her fantasies; to indulge and partake vicariously through her novels and clandestine porn watching. She may even act it out in real life, with a daring sexual rendezvous... or simply with her vibrator.

## THE BIG BAD WOLF

Historically, women were perceived to be *evil* and the cause of man's eternal *strife*. This may be true and is exactly why she's so significant. A woman will either enhance a man's life or destroy it. This is her *gift* to him or a *curse*. Her role is to test what is laid before her. Whatever is weak or inauthentic will crumble under her provocation. She's the big bad wolf who'll blow your house down if it isn't built strong enough. Lesser men call her wicked because they don't understand her purpose. A strong woman will challenge a man to be his best, she needs to know *who he is* before investing in him. Weak men will cower and project insults, call her crazy, evil and an unstable drama queen. He does so because he isn't up to the task and *she knows it.* Unconsciously, she'll also deny her part in adding to the *drama or problem.* She'll play the victim and degrade him; he'll grow even angrier. Spineless men need not apply. She wants a strong man *to rise and take control.*

Her *undesirable behaviour* is the direct result of his *leadership* or lack of it. The chaos results from his inability to guide her and his lack of self-control. Inherently, she wants to be vulnerable, but only if his *purpose and direction* are strong enough. He can't fake it, because she will feel it. A woman will test her man to see if she can trust his leadership; she wants to know if he can be easily swayed or controlled. When he passes, she should never insult him further by continuing to make him jump through more hoops. If he's dominant, she'll submit to his leadership naturally and willingly. However, if he isn't or cannot guide her, she'll find another who is. She may settle because she truly loves him, or because, she has no other options. A good woman who loves her man unconditionally will remain and help him be his best. *Behind every successful man is a good woman.*

A woman is designed to *receive* and *amplify*; she incubates and grows. She doesn't give back what she's given... she *transforms it.* The only thing you get back is the length of your penis you put inside her, *but she'll take your balls if you let her.*

"Give her sperm, she produces a baby. Give her a house, she gives you a home. Give her food and she provides a meal. Grind her with frustration... and she'll make your life a living hell." She can make your journey an enjoyable one or a fucking nightmare. Her *emotional storms* and *turbulent waves* can wreak havoc on your boat and even capsize it. A good woman will provide you with smooth sailing over calm waters and enrich your journey. If you don't like what you're *getting,* then change what you're *giving.*

Feminine energy will amplify the masculine spirit, whether it's negative or positive. This will greatly affect *her and his* life; she needs to be careful who she lets pervade her. Ladies, make sure his wounds have healed before engaging, or you'll make them worse. A toxic man also has the power to destroy you. He can erode your radiance, confidence, self-love and respect. When there's harmony, he'll love, lead and protect you. In turn, you'll trust, respect and follow him. What you do for each other, you do for *both of you.* You can tell the amount of respect a woman has for her man by the level of compliance she shows him. The more resistant and defiant she is, the less respect she has for him.

## WEATHERING HER STORM

Since time began, women have been angry at men for one reason or another. Most guys don't know why or know how to solve this. Women have awoken and now feel the freedom to express this rage. They're no longer hiding; they have found their voice. Women can be destructive if they're restricted or left unbridled. Most will repress their fear of abandonment, judgements and anger, *and the pressure builds.* When she can't take it any longer, she explodes; *the facade has crumbled.* This explosion is her defence mechanism and her need to protect herself and her heart. The outburst is her last line of protection. The majority of guys don't know how to react when this happens. Insecure men will compensate by being too nice, or an asshole. Instead of facing her full-on, they'll try to control, gaslight or manipulate her... making her crazier. A man needs to establish boundaries when he encounters this behaviour.

What if she blows a fuse and goes all Kali on you? If you re-member in chapter one, she's the warrioress wife of Lord Shiva. For those familiar with this Hindu mythos, Kali began killing many demons and went mad with blood lust. In doing so, she almost destroyed the world and her hubby. Many believe it was Kali who tamed Shiva, but it was he who tamed her. Women will shit-test men and look for boundaries to see how safe they are with them; they want to know what they can get away with. Sometimes her rage is simply chaos fuelled by a deep trauma, or it can an addiction to the *adrenaline rush* of being *set off.* No matter how spiteful, bitchy or tough she appears, underneath is a little girl with insecurities you know nothing about. Each time a man fails her or runs away from her wrath *is more evidence for her to believe she's unlovable.*

When you support her and offer her the space to heal, you're helping resolve her deepest fears of *abandonment and oppression.* Surrender isn't always beautiful, it will take a strong man to withstand the release of all the darkness and chaos buried with-in her. She will shake, cry, yell, convulse and attack you as she purges all her repressed anger and pain trapped inside. You'll face all the evil that's blocked her from feeling loved. How you handle this will expose your true colours; this strength can't be faked.

You'll need superhuman resilience to carry and lead her out of her emotional hell fury. She'll blame you for being the cause of her pain while expecting you to lead her out. Nevertheless, you can't provoke her any further, or she'll attack like a scorpion and inflict a thousand more stings upon you. In doing so, you'll have to show her you won't tolerate her abuse. This is a tall task, and I feel for any man who takes this on. Surrendering into her heart will feel like her death, and is why she'll resist. Say, *"Trust me, babe, I'll catch you. Stop blaming me. I don't deserve this and have every reason to leave, but I'm staying because I love you."*

Never tell a woman to *relax* when she's on fire, nor try to edit her emotions. Sure it makes sense to your rational mind, but to her, it's an additional trigger. Weather her storm, but don't be her emotional toilet or cesspool; this means holding her hair without letting her puke on you. You'll need to stay calm, stern yet soft, have faith in her and be patient, or she'll see you're not in control. *Love her, but not her actions.* Lay down your arms and *let it play out.* This doesn't mean surrendering or being passive. You're not to fix her; *guide her objectivity.*

She'll try anything to force you to bail on her so she can validate her unworthiness. If you remain, she may try harder to sabotage your relationship, but stand firm. When a woman knows she's dealing with an authentically strong man, she'll soften and begin to feel safe. She can be herself, wild and vulnerable. The little girl within her will remember *she is lovable.*

I caution you, once her bitching stops, she's stopped caring, and you may have lost her forever. Men interpret this as if *everything is finally okay or she's come around.* When and if she no longer reacts, she has stopped investing in you. So nagging can be a good thing as there's still time to course-correct. Usually, she'll exhaust every option before totally shutting down. So pay attention, because she'll try to fix the relationship before deciding to abandon it. Women are more receptive to problems well before men notice, by then, it's usually too late. Having said that, there's an exception. Isn't there always? Women with an inflated sense of value, *a Stacy,* or those having more resources available to upgrade... *will.* Those without better options, who feel insecure or truly love their guy, will do everything in their power to save the relationship and make it work.

## TRAGIC MIRROR ON THE WALL

Unless a woman is a self-deluded-only-fan-spicy-content-influencer believing the inflated value given to her by approval-seeking beta fans, she may suffer from insecurities guys will never understand. Women are naturally humble, and they need constant reassurance to feel valued and beautiful. This built-in humility forces them to notice every flaw regardless of how hot they are. If you think she's *a ten,* she'll see *eleven* imperfections.

Women aren't wired like men; they don't look in the mirror and say, *"Hey stud, how you doin?"* as he overlooks his beer belly, small dick, protruding nose hair, uncut toenails and other conspicuous shortcomings. The more beautiful she is, the worse her self-critique can be. She can have a million likes on her social media, and they won't be enough. Ultimately, the only *like* that matters is her own.

Nonetheless, make her feel special, tell her and show how beautiful she is... *every single day.* She needs constant reminders, and no, *it doesn't get old.* Just don't overdo the compliments. Ironically, complimenting may backfire when you first meet her. Get to know her before you carry out the pedestal. Men don't understand the pressures women face, those imposed on them by the media and the fashion industry. The so-called *role models* have undergone enhancements and plastic surgery, not to mention Photoshop. Who created these unrealistic benchmarks anyway? I think some of these women are really *skinny dudes* in disguise. Beauty isn't about analyzing a person; instead, focus on how they make you feel. This is the same when admiring a rose or any flower. When you look at it you notice its beauty and how it radiates. The moment you begin analyzing, you stop admiring it and see only flaws. Your focus switches from wholeness to individual facets like lines and age spots; *it stops being a beautiful flower.*

I remember when I bought a diamond to design an engagement ring for my then-wife. I used to stare at it all the time. One night while looking at it under bright light, I saw something horrifying. The next day I called the jeweller and asked him why the diamond had an unsightly line. He assured me it was a natural process—when diamonds are formed deep within the Earth, they develop natural birthmarks called inclusions. I seriously considered returning it and buying a flawless cubic zirconia instead. I understand why plastic surgery is a thing, but for me, natural beauty outshines all. Did you know most men prefer women who wear less makeup? Interestingly, in Italian, makeup is called *trucco,* which also means *trick.*

Women are programmed to believe abusive treatment is their fault. This sounds like an oxymoron, but guys, hear me out. She may not admit it or openly take responsibility, but she'll wonder what she did wrong to upset you. She'll question everything instead of why you're being an asshole. If you cut her, she'll apologize for bleeding on the floor. Many women will make excuses for men and stay in toxic relationships longer than they should. Maybe if she improves, becomes more valuable, prettier or smarter, he may change back to how it was in the beginning.

## WOMEN NEED TO FEEL SAFE

*"Crocodiles are easy. They try to kill you and eat you. People are harder. Sometimes they pretend to be your friend first."* ~ Steve Irwin. I'm not telling you to become an alligator and terrorize people. Unlike most animals, humans are *unreliable*; they say one thing and do another. This isn't safe, especially for women. Being congruent means your *thoughts, feelings and actions* are in alignment, always and in all ways… *consistently.*

*"A rose creates thorns to protect itself"*~Luther Burbank. This American botanist created over *eight hundred* varieties of plant strains and produced at least *sixty types* of spineless cacti. So guys, don't expect her to drop her *bitch thorns* if you keep acting like a *prick*. Most men don't realize how many women have been overpowered and sexually violated. They fail to understand the power imbalance and how it puts them at a disadvantage; in a physical sense and dangerous situations. They don't feel the anxiety she suffers by constantly having to be on high alert. Guys can't relate unless they've experienced this firsthand. Imagine being in jail; you're naked in the shower, and accidentally drop the soap. *Two hundred and fifty pound* Bubba and his meathead friends take a liking to you… Capeesh?

Now imagine the daily fear of having to share your rendezvous location with your friends before meeting up with a new guy, carry whistles and mace spray in your purse, walk with your keys in hand in a way they can be used as a weapon if necessary, park under well-lit areas, huddle with a pack of friends for your safety, be afraid whenever you're alone, pretend to be on your phone when harassed, give a fake name and number, pretend to have boyfriends and wearing fake wedding rings, cover your drink at bars or parties to avoid getting drugged, stay aloof so you can't be read, remain silent when verbally harassed to avoid violence or an attack; act happy and confident when you're really afraid, so you don't come across as a bitch, fear being raped, withhold information, not criticize men because you're afraid they may seriously hurt or kill you, be mindful of wearing provocative attire, keep quiet when guys are objectifying you instead of admiring your beauty, defuse macho and domineering behaviour... *just to name a few.*

These examples are obvious, but what about the more obscure? Like when a guy texts a woman, "Hey..." followed by nothing. This can freak her out or be triggering because it's creepy and ambiguous. If you're going to slide her a direct message or cold approach her on the street, make certain you're *clear on your intentions.* Sure, a bit of shyness is cute and endearing, but if it makes her feel uneasy, *then no.* Being nervous, vague, wishy-washy or contradicting may scare her, even if you don't mean to. So will being *super nice* and pretending you're not interested in her sexually. She'll wonder what your intentions are. *"What does he want? Why is he being sneaky about it?"*

Different women have told me the same thing countless times, "When guys first text me they're so nice, but the moment I make it clear I'm not interested, they freak out and call me a whore, a tease or a fucking bitch." Also saying, "I love you" right after the second date is another *red flag.* She'll wonder how easily you can fall out of love as soon as another woman comes along. She doesn't want a rudderless boat or a moth to the flame.

"Do you know why women fake orgasms? Because they think guys give a shit." This may be a joke men tell each other, but if it was true, why do guys ask if they made her cum? If she's faking it, there's a reason and it's not always about you. Sure, it could be because you suck in bed and she doesn't want to hurt your feelings. If you feel inadequate, get over it, you need to consider why she's stroking your delicate ego. She may be protecting herself and is afraid of upsetting you. You can seriously hurt her because you felt rejected; she doesn't want to be left vulnerable. She may also suffer from abandonment issues, trauma, or not being good enough. At least you got laid, *consider yourself lucky.*

## SCARING HER AWAY

Since I'm naturally empathic, I had to learn how to stay grounded when I was around women I liked. I also had to be mindful not to fall into my feminine energy, or take on hers. When they were feeling anxious or nervous, I'd feel it and absorb their anxiety. In turn, they'd feel it off of me; this would create a biofeedback loop and it would escalate. This made them feel unsafe. Until I learned how to stand in my power, *I wasn't safe.*

Physical boundaries were also something I learned. Being Italian, touchy feeling is par for the course, so I didn't realize this made some women very uncomfortable. I never groped any private parts inappropriately or unsolicited. Some women can't even be touched on their arm, if anywhere at all. Eventually, I figured out where and when to touch them, the safe areas and no-fly zones. I also learned how to respect the more subtle boundaries, those which apply to every living thing, human and animal. Those beyond the physical; the *spatial and the energetic.*

We all have personal space and don't like when others encroach on it. How do you feel when you're in a crowded elevator or when someone is close talking with you? Uneasy right? Be mindful when approaching others, don't invade their space or aura. You can make a woman feel quite uncomfortable if you penetrate her energetic field. Avoid doing so, unless there's an invitation. You can make her feel nervous by coming on *too strong* and also by appearing *too weak.* Women need to feel safe not only on a physical level but psychologically and emotionally as well… unequivocally.

Guys, you can scare a woman away by your needing her approval, placating and acquiescing, being insecure, not standing up for what you want, cowering to rejection, caving in when the going gets tough, oversharing your emotions and feelings, being vague and a conciliating yes man, blaming and gaslighting her; your tone of voice, and by your lack of empathy. *Once you lose her trust, it will be hard getting it back.*

Women say they want an emotional man but don't understand what it truly means. Yes, she wants him to feel his emotions, but not to be taken hostage by them. If he's emotional, he's dangerous, because along with the sensitivity and crying comes rage, fear and jealousy. If she tilts like a pinball machine and he's not emotionally strong, things can get ugly really fast. If he's easily affected by her emotions or his own, it shows he can be controlled and easily manipulated. An emotional man makes her feel icky and unsafe. She doesn't want the responsibility of dealing with his feelings; that's his job. *She isn't his mother.*

Guys, make sure your *boundaries* are *strong* and your *expectations* are *clear* and know what your *purpose* is. You need to be emotionally centred, have strong leadership skills, and be all in with her. Create a safe container, stand firm and be unwavering. You have to meet her at every level. The only way she'll feel safe in her body is when you are grounded firmly in yours. Breathe deeply into your being so she follows; this will help bring her back into her body. Breathe with her, meet her, and lead her back into her heart. She needs to know and feel that she can trust you, and is emotionally and physically safe with you... *completely.*

She needs your authenticity, acceptance, connection, presence, non-judgement and respect. She wants to be honoured, desired, cherished and loved. When she knows your heart is open and you're invested, she will feel safe enough to drop her defences and surrender to love... and to you. Make her feel safe, and understand her depth, her power, her sexuality and her purpose. *Never take her for granted.*

# CHAPTER TEN

# WHAT SHE WANTS

## WHAT DOES SHE WANT?

Like plenty of men, what they *can't have.* We want what others want and have. Many of us suffer from shiny toy syndrome; wanting the latest and greatest until something better comes along. We want something because we don't have it, but once we get it we don't want it anymore. We're like babies with our toys; we'll play with something until we get bored of it, then discard it when it loses its lustre. That's until our friend, toddler-toy-taker picks it up. Suddenly, it becomes our favourite toy again, and we snatch it back. *"You can't play with it, it's mine!"* Just like our exes, they're not supposed to move on and find someone better than us. Yet, it's ok if they downgrade... right?

Wanting something we don't have isn't a male or female thing, it's human nature. However, men will argue women are guilty of not knowing what they want, *but wanting it now.* I believe *women do know what they want,* but it's to their advantage to pretend they don't. This keeps them safe and evasive, *but it drives guys insane.* Women would rather be accused of being indecisive than have to pay the price for a bad decision.

## THE HUSBAND AND WOMEN STORE

Once upon a time, there was a very smart entrepreneur. He opened a store that gave away husbands to single women who wanted to get married. This was a cutting-edge idea that made him extremely wealthy. Women had to submit a non-refundable deposit of $50.00 before entering. There was a sign by the entrance with instructions each shopper had to obey.

*"You may only visit this store once. There are six floors to choose from; you may select any male from that level. If you aren't satisfied with any of the choices, you may go up to the next floor. Please note; you cannot go back down to any of the previous floors; you'll need to exit the building immediately. Thank you, good luck and enjoy your shopping."*

A woman goes into the store. On the first floor, the sign reads, *"Men who have good jobs."* She decides to pass and go up to the next floor. *"Men who have great jobs and love children."* She thinks about it for a second and decides, "Hmm, I'll go up to the third floor." *"Men who have amazing jobs, love children and are good-looking."* "Wow, look at all the hot and successful men here." Still, she feels compelled to keep going, so up to the fourth floor she goes. The sign reads, *"Men who earn six figures, adore children, are very handsome and do housework."* "OMG, this is incredible, I can hardly stand it. And there are two more floors left!" Nonetheless, she goes up one more floor. *"Multimillionaires, adores children, drop-dead gorgeous, fit, enjoys doing housework naked, well hung and great in bed."* She can't contain herself, and is tempted to stay... but cannot help but go to the sixth floor.

*"Welcome to the sixth and final floor. You are visitor number 81,456,009. There are no men here. This floor exists only to prove you're impossible to please. Thank you for shopping at the Husband Store. Kindly leave through the yellow door on your left."*

Now to avoid discrimination and gender bias, the store owner also opened up The Wife Store right across the street. On the wall was a similar set of instructions; it also had six floors. The first floor read, *"Women who love sex."* The second floor read, *"Women who love sex and have big boobs."*

Interestingly, no one knows what was on the *third, fourth, fifth and sixth floors* because they've never been visited.

## HYPERGAMY

That was just a joke, but there's truth to it. Women are wired to find the best option available to ensure their innate need for *protection and survival.* Financial security is one of the main drivers of female *hypergamy.* The words *hyper and hypo* mean *above and below* respectively; and the word *gamos* in Greek means *marriage. Hyper*gamy is when a person marries or forms a sexual relationship with another having a higher or similar background; this includes financial, sociological and education-al status. *Hypo*gamy is the opposite and means marrying across or below one's status. *Women* tend to be more *hypergamous* and *men hypogamous.*

Men are attracted to physical features rather than status or financial class. He's more concerned with a woman's youth, fertility and her looks over how much she makes, or has ac-quired materially. Women are attracted to higher-value men; security, experience, high-status, influence, power, resources and wealth. Sadly, if a man has no *equity,* it doesn't matter how nice he is. Sorry guys, it's hardwired and may be the reason she rejects, dumps or cheats on you. Since men aren't attracted to high-achieving women, they too may leave or have an affair with a woman who is less driven and more feminine. My apologies, once more to the ladies.

According to a 2016 study conducted by the University of British Columbia, more women are earning university degrees than men. *Ninety-three percent* are likely to marry guys who earn a higher income. I'm not a math expert, but as more women become independent and successful, the odds of finding a compatible partner are dwindling. *Men need to raise the bar, or women need to lower theirs.* Since they can't, due to their nature, it's a problem that's not going away. Hypergamy not only leaves succesful women single, but it attracts narcissists. The average Joe with a regular job is less driven and more laid-back. Most men feel inferior to partners who make more than them, which increases their stress and anxiety.

Justified or not, unabashed hypergamous women get labelled as gold diggers. But the fact is, *most* women are hypergamous on some level, and it doesn't matter how high their status is. Of course, this isn't true *for all* women. Hypergamy doesn't care about a guy's feelings or his struggles; it waits at the finish line for the winner. Women don't care *how* you got there; they care that you *did.* It's not about the car or job you have, as they only *represent* the *discipline and labour* it took to get them. Not everyone can get to the top or buy such a car. If it was easy, then everyone would do it. This is like buying a woman flowers; it's not about the bouquet itself, it's the thought behind it—*the reason for giving it.*

Gold digger prank videos have been flooding the scene lately. A dude walks up to a hot chick wearing cheap clothing, or stands beside a crappie car and asks her out. She rejects him and says she has a boyfriend or is busy. Cue in the plot twist, he comes back driving a Lamborghini—his cell phone suddenly rings, he lands the million-dollar deal—his lawyer calls and says he's to collect an inheritance. Magically her boyfriend disappears and her calendar has suddenly freed up. She's eager to join him for dinner and asks to get into the supercar. Then the guy rejects her and calls her out for being a gold digger; she goes ballistic. *I think these videos are staged.*

## WOMEN DON'T WANT NICE GUYS

You're hanging out with a girl you like and she says you're a great guy. *"Any girl will be lucky to have you. You're my BFF."* She gives you hugs and even lets you sleep beside her, but *no sex of course.* You're her rock, she dumps all of her problems on you, cries on your shoulder and tells you how rotten her boyfriend is treating her. Ya, the guy she's having sex with. You're confused, and wonder why she doesn't see you're the guy she truly needs. *I'm nice and would never treat you as badly as he does. I'm right here beside you... Why can't you see me? Why do you keep going back to that jerk? He treats you like shit!* This doesn't make any sense to you, but for her... it does.

We've all heard women want nice guys, and they'll even confirm this, *but then go after the jerk.* She'll be nice to you, and you'll think it's because she wants you... *nope.* No matter how nice you are or how hard you try, you're staying in her friend zone little buddy. You have no game, and you do too much for her... you're her doormat. In her eyes, you're boring and predictable, bland and saltless. No matter how healthy she *wants* to eat, she's *craving* junk food. You're constantly getting curved; this is when someone rejects you so sneakily that you don't even know you're getting rejected. If you could just be more of an asshole and stopped trying so hard to impress her; you may have better results… but it's not in your nature.

Sometimes, life hardens us and forces our hand—it happened to me. *I was the once nice guy gone bad,* one of many good men destroyed by a bitch… or four. Being a prick went against every fibre of my being, but it also sucked feeling like a gay best friend. You can continue being the nice guy, getting led on and walked over, or become an angry asshole—you could play the victim and join a men's support group, or do neither. Instead, you can decide to *take responsibility and grow some balls.*

After countless rejections and betrayals, many guys give up and join movements like Men Going Their Own Way (MGTOW) and Men's Rights Activists (MRA). Perhaps you're still a virgin or an angry Incel hating on those who are having sex… *and lots of it.* These types of men have turned *toxic* and *misogynistic;* they've become fearful and angry toward women. This is no different from the *venomous misandry* spewed by Neo-feminists who support the subjugation and hatred of men. For every eternal bachelor, player and pick-up artist is a guy suffering from a *broken heart.* Maybe, he's just had enough of the games and women's ambiguous nature. Only you can decide if you want to continue being invisible and be taken advantage of. You can change this, or you can keep waiting… *maybe* the right one will come along… *eventually.* And if she does, chances are she'll get bored of you quickly… and move on.

## BEING NICE ISN'T AN ENTITLEMENT

Just because you're nice to her, buy her dinner, listen to her problems and become her teddy bear to cry on; *does not entitle you to anything.* Sex isn't a right you should be given because you're polite or kiss her ass with compliments. This puts undue pressure on her, it's an unfair obligation... and it's *dishonourable.* I get it, your frustration and loneliness are valid, but that's not her fault. Stop playing the victim, you just don't make her wet, it's that simple. She loves sex and probably has lots of it, but just not with you. Stop getting angry and *calling her a bitch* because you couldn't manipulate her into getting what you wanted. In high school, we used to call the girls who had sex with everyone *sluts,* and the ones who slept with everyone *except you,* we called *bitches.* See, you're not such a nice guy after all, are you?

Stop being her white knight, she doesn't need your heroics. *Saviours* overcompensate and give unsolicited defence in the hopes she will reciprocate with sex or romantic interest. Nice guys may think it's the jerks who are oppressing and taking advantage of women, when in fact, *they're the guilty ones.* Women are not your therapist or your mommy, so don't unload on them like they are. Never be emotional in front of them. If you need to, go somewhere in the forest and cry under a tree. Drink with your buddies, seek counsel, go to a therapist or find a men's group and talk it out. Being too emotional will repulse any attraction she may have for you. She'll feel uncomfortable, it's not her responsibility; she's not your nurse. That's on you. Get your shit together and stop whimpering. Grow a pair, unless, of course, you want to be friend-zoned... *forever.*

*Note:* There's a myth about why guys commit suicide. Many believe it's because they've been taught not to cry or had to hold their emotions in. *False.* Those who take their life do so not from emotional repression, but from feeling disempowered. They're unable to take control or responsibility for their emotions. They've let the world bully them and are unable to fight back.

Nice guys are flat, uneasy, awkward, powerless, fearful, reactive and agreeable around women. They are submissive and people-pleasing. Dominant men are the opposite; most times women don't even phase them.

There's a difference between *doing things* for a woman, versus, *overcompensating* to gain her approval. A dominant man will change because he wants to, for himself first. This eventually benefits her and he knows it—*devotion.* The emasculated man changes for her acceptance—*submission.* She doesn't like *agreeable yes men* waiting at her beck and call. Stop trying to be her girlfriend because she has enough already. She also has her cats and her gay boyfriend she can hug and get advice from. Unless, of course, you want to replace them.

One day you'll realize you can do almost anything you want to a woman and get away with it; *just don't make her bored.* Avoid slipping into the friend's zone and compromising sexual tension. She's attracted to jerks over you because *they're not boring or trying to be her friend—there's lust.* A woman can love a guy but not be in love with him. You may be wondering, "What's the difference? That's like telling your bank I have debt with you, but I'm not in debt with you, so I'll stop making payments." What this means is she has to *respect you* more than she *loves you.* She may *hate* the jerk, but she *respects* him and that's worth way more.

## WOMEN LOVE JERKS

This is a misnomer as women don't love jerks, her *biology* does. You see, an asshole is closer to what she needs than a nice guy is. Women would rather try to tame a *mustang* than attempt to fire up a docile *pony*. Domesticating a *jerk* is more feasible than trying to unbridle a simp—*the nice guy.* Women also believe they can change a man. I've never understood this... weren't they initially attracted to him for how he was?

What do the bad boy, rock star and billionaire all have in common? *They do what they want, when they want and how they want.* They can get whatever they need simply by expressing their desire for it, and they make no apologies. This is why a vampire is so powerful and seductive. Imagine how alluring Dracula would be if he was insecure or had to ask permission before biting a woman's neck.

Most romance novels and Literotica stories are based on these types of characters. These *dangerous men* choose the women they want on their terms. Women are faced with a dilemma; how to benefit from their power without being harmed by it. She wants her King Kong, someone who can dominate the world yet is the focus of his desire so he can protect her. She wants a jerk who has chosen to be nice to her exclusively; *this is the nice guy she wants.* Many times this backfires. She may, or may not be aware of the potential risks. Such a man can physically dominate her with his strength, end up in jail, have an alcohol or drug problem, be less likely to compliment her and may leave her as a single mom. Nonetheless, she'll take that chance over a man who doesn't have any backbone at all.

You'd be surprised at how many women send letters and marriage proposals to convicts (even serial killers) in jail. Granted, a large percentage of their admirers have had prior abuse or suffer from some form of trauma. There's also a sense of safety when communicating from the outside, which encourages their perception of having control. I'm not telling you to become a criminal or a jerk, *just grow some balls.* If you can't be that guy, stop complaining about women who want them.

Women who prefer jerks are swimming in a sea of simps. She only notices the sharks and not the plethora of neighbouring shrimp—*soon to be its food.* What a woman says she wants and what she actually does are two different things. Remember, *don't listen to her words—watch her actions.* She'll deny wanting a jerk, and feminized men will believe her. That's why they'll try to protect her from the assholes she complains about. Yet are shocked to see her run right into their arms. *She wants to want a nice guy, but can't help herself.* I believe women who say they want nice men is true to a point. They want *just nice enough* to indicate he's not a heartless bastard, at least to her.

Women only make *rules* for *beta* males, but they'll be quick to break them for the guys they really want. She'll be busy, have a boyfriend or have to wash her hair when *simp-man* calls. When Chad texts her, she'll sell her tickets to the Bon Jovi concert, or invite him to come along. She'll tell her girlfriend to sit this one out. She'll sexually *hold out* on the good guys, but quickly will *put out* for Chad, *to keep him interested.* The sad thing is he doesn't care about her and will bounce after getting laid.

Women who love *bad boys* have terrible filters or may have unhealed wounds. They pick the wrong guy, get hurt and then blame him for being narcissistic, or an asshole. It's like putting your hand in the fire and complaining it hurts, but then you keep doing it. This boggles the minds of good guys as they see it play out all so *predictably.* She'll choose the dude who's rebellious, emotionally unavailable and selfish; then can't understand why she ends up alone, single with his child, heartbroken or going to therapy. Nice guys generally stick around and want to be in their child's life. They won't bail on a woman if he knocks her up. They'll offer child support and will help in any way they can. Good guys don't take a woman's money, energy, time, or the worst offence... *they don't play with her heart.*

Here's the thing, although jerks are self-serving, they're congruent and *not wishy-washy.* Ironically, she feels safer with them over a nervous and pandering nice guy. *Bad boys aren't boring.*

## FACTA NON-VERBA

This Latin phrase means; *acts not words.* What she says she *wants* is different from what she *needs.* She's powerless against her nature; hypergamy and her need for survival override her fairytale programming. She wants a man who she can't push around. If *she can then anyone can,* and she no longer feels safe with him. A dominant man cannot be governed unless it's his choice. Whereas the nice guy doesn't want to rock the boat, he'll acquiesce. Whenever a simp is disrespected, whether it's on purpose or not, he'll feel it too petty to address. He'll gaslight himself and will override his instincts to make himself wrong so he won't appear uncaring. In doing so, she loses her respect for him. I believe if given the chance, a woman would pick a caveman over the modern-day man.

A study was done by showing women pictures of smiling and non-smiling men on dating apps. They were asked who they found more attractive. As you've probably guessed, the majority picked the non-smilers. Some women stated, over smiling men reek of desperation. Ironically, it was the men who were more attracted to the smiling women. A similar study was done on men in regard to facial hair. It turned out, more women favoured the beard over the cleanly shaven, with an exception. Since women are attracted to rarity, their favour will change depending on the trend. If every guy sported a beard, her preference would shift to clean-cut. Women prefer wolves, not the safety-seeking sheep following the herd.

*Question;* Your woman works in an office where there are men. She's *always complimenting* how great a guy Bob is. At the same time, she's *constantly complaining* about what an asshole Frank is. Which guy should you be more worried about? I'm sure by now you know the answer. If not, you need to reread this chapter because it's obvious you haven't been following. *I believe hating someone is an unconscious attraction.* If you didn't care about a person, why would their actions bother you?

This reminds me of high school. Beta-boy Bob asks Susie to the prom, she says yes. He buys flowers, champagne, and a tuxedo, rents the limo and hotel room. *"Aww you're so sweet,"* she says as she jumps into Chad's car after the dance. They both go to make out point and have sex in the back seat of his car. Bobby sits alone in the hotel room and drinks all the champagne; he's feeling sad, angry, destitute and confused. The flowers left behind begin to wilt... and the drooping petals weep, "She loves me not."

Women will lose interest in yes men who always give in to their whims. She wants her man's purpose to be greater than her changing moods. She wants him to say "No" to her sometimes. Guys, don't give her what she *wants—give* her what she *needs.* Let her know *you chose to invest in her;* she's part of your mission, not the centre of your universe. Women are attracted to men who know they can have other women; look at ugly rock stars. The biggest turn-off for women is knowing a guy is needy and afraid of losing them. She wants to *know he chose her out of all his other options. She wants to feel special.* Remember, women are aroused by being desired.

Choose her and make her feel wanted above all others. Ironically, by not showing any interest, she'll wonder why you're not drooling over her as every other guy does.

## YOU'RE NOT READY FOR HIM

I digress... You may say you're ready for the guy you want, but you're not. If this were true, you'd already be with him. Secretly, you crave a man you can't control or wrap around your finger (that's reserved for daddy). You realize you can't handle such a man, so you go after those who are safer and more malleable. We both know how this ends; he's fine until you get bored or frustrated. Then you leave or cheat on him because he's not what you really want.

You fear the guy who demands more of you, who asks you to go deeper and give more than you've ever given anyone else. Instead of having the courage to totally surrender, you yo-yo between the *nice guy* and the *emotionally unavailable asshole* who doesn't give a shit about you. Staying on the surface is safer than journeying deep into your soul. The man you *truly need* won't put up with your half-assed effort because you're afraid of getting hurt and unwilling to open your heart. No, he'll make you accountable and will call you out on your bullshit. *Women who want vulnerable men want to control them.* A dominant man won't put up with it and will demand you give up your need for control. He will also dismiss your ambiguity. You want such a man, but due to your wounds... *you're too afraid.*

You say you're happy with what you got, but why are you constantly complaining? You choose to play the victim, you're addicted to the drama and everything is always wrong. You moan because he's not challenging you; he's predictable, immature, unfulfilling... *and not taking you deeper.* If you're not happy, then leave and cut the BS.

You keep dating losers and blame them for it. Instead, ask yourself, Why am I always attracting the *wieners* and not the *winners?* I understand your dilemma; if you can control a guy or manipulate him into giving you what you want, you can't totally trust him. If you can't trust him, you won't feel safe. You want a guy who can take the lead, but you don't want to give up your control. The question is, "Are you ready for such a man?"

# CHAPTER ELEVEN

# ARE YOU TOXIC?

## BORN THIS WAY?

I don't believe anyone is born toxic unless they're a natural psychopath. Life experience shapes us whether it's been good or bad. These conditions build our story and our ego. The effects of these events can cause us to develop passive or domineering characteristics. These early childhood occurrences are responsible for unbalancing our masculine and feminine polarities and for creating unhealthy behaviour; which affects our relationships. Life changes us; we adapt the best we can. Women shouldn't be blamed for turning masculine, nor men for becoming passive. Social pressure and the need to compensate for the ever-changing roles are partly responsible; allowing it to happen is the most paramount. During this process, women have turned into *warriors and* men have become *pussies*. Guys are letting women castrate them and acquiesce by gift-wrapping their balls.

Everyone is frustrated and we're blaming each other for the mess we're creating. It's always the other person's fault, nobody wants to hold themselves accountable. Our current social narrative is holding this inversion in place, it has become normalized, and questioning it will get you in hot water. This illusion is propped up not only by twisted perceptions but by the need to protect our egos—mostly at the expense of gaslighting others. *Only a toxic person can make another believe they're holding a grudge when they're just maintaining their boundary.*

People's *feelings* matter more now than *facts* do. We're blackmailed and called bigots by those who get *offended easily.* We are shamed by those who cannot regulate their emotions and are out of touch with reality. The lines are becoming blurred and clarity is lost. We've become a *feels before reals* society. The lack of love and respect we have for ourselves is lowering our tolerance for disrespect. We're too afraid to stand up and establish our boundaries.

When shown respect, we feel valued. Men need to feel admired, women need to feel loved. These qualities are not demanded, but freely given. Respect is earned, but not through compliance. A woman saying, *"I'll give him respect when he earns it"* is no different from him saying, *"I'll give her love when she earns it."* Disrespect and toxic behaviour are destroying our relationships and are keeping us single. Men are being dishonoured and women are equally disgraced. We've got to stop this bullshit.

## IS SHE REALLY A BITCH?

I once made the coldest woman cry in my arms, after I called her out on her behaviour. Most men's reaction to a cold or negative response from a woman is to cower or take offence and call her a bitch. I was guilty of both more than once in the past. The one time I did turn the tables was at a bar. I had my share of liquid courage and a chip on my shoulder that night. An attractive woman was standing alone in front of me. So, I hit on her. I began chatting her up, but she didn't want any part of it. She attempted to bust my chops and very aggressively at that. In a condescending tone, she said, *I'm not here to pick up desperate drunk dudes, so don't waste my time.* Usually, this would have set me back and off to the corner to lick my wounds, but what I did next, surprised even me.

I looked deeply into her eyes and said, "Sweetie, we both know this bitchy crap is bullshit. I know deep down you're a sensitive little girl who's very afraid and hurt right now. I don't know what happened, and it's not any of my business. You are a grown woman, this bratty behaviour may have worked when you were six, but your temper tantrum shit won't fly with me. I don't deserve to be disrespected like this. I'm being nice, and we're in a bar for fuck's sake. Stay home if you don't want anyone hitting on you. Now say sorry and stop being a little brat." She was silent, I could see she was going to cry. Instinctively, I gave her a playful hug. She began balling her eyes out and shared some painful experiences she was going through. She was having a bad night; it had nothing to do with me.

Most times, *bitchy* is a smoke screen, just like *domineering* is in a man. Both are born from pain. I fully understand the need to protect yourself, but it should never be at the expense of another. I'm not suggesting you call anyone out as I did with the woman at the bar because you can be dealing with a very wounded person. You need compassion, but without being a doormat.

## SHADOW POSSESSED

According to psychologist Carl Jung, the *Amina* is the feminine part of a man's personality; the *Animus* is the masculine part of a woman's. Our shadow self (our hidden aspects) breaks up into the Anima and Animus. Jung believed, once males developed their masculine aspect, they could expand and integrate their feminine and vice versa for women. In early childhood formation and for social acceptance, boys are taught to suppress their feminine side and girls their masculine. These undeveloped aspects get buried in our *shadow self.* They aren't expressed because they're considered inappropriate behaviour in society. Whatever is ignored, festers and can become potentially fatal, and able to possess or control us like an invisible puppet master.

Girls need to be caring and compassionate; aggression and assertiveness are behaviours reserved for boys. Jung believes women who are argumentative and confrontational are considered Animus possessed and men who are passive and succumb to their emotions are Anima possessed. When we get stuck in our masculine and feminine polarities without developing and integrating the opposite polarity, we can become toxic. Inversion, imbalance and depolarization occur. As we get older, we're afforded more resources to explore and integrate our suppressed masculine and feminine energies. Ironically, as women age, they become more assertive and men lose their drive.

There's a difference between masculine, *masculinized*, feminine and *feminized*. One is *authentic* and the other is a toxic veneer *pretending to be.* You can appear to be masculine or feminine, but they're simply masks, which can be worn overtop of each other.

Girls are generally born with a dominant feminine polarity. However, if mom teaches her to be independent and not need a man, or if dad's influence was toxic, she may become *masculinized*. Trauma may also induce a masculine persona, which may override her innate feminine side. She develops this to protect herself. She may learn to act feminine to fit into society by mirroring the femininity exhibited in other women. Her natural feminine polarity was traumatized into becoming masculine, and to compensate, she wears a feminized mask over that to appear feminine.

Conversely, boys are typically born with a dominant masculine polarity. They can become *feminized* by a toxic dad, trauma, or an over-coddling, or an over-bearing mother. They'll try to please others because they've become feminized. Since he isn't getting laid, he will learn to disguise himself as being masculine. He wears a masculinized camouflage over his feminized masculinity. This is how toxicity behaviour is created. *Multilayered masks.*

The goal is to maintain the polarization *(opposition)* of the masculine and feminine poles while preserving the balance in each. Healthy masculine and feminine energies are in equilibrium with one another. When out of balance, we can fall into one of their extremes—*codependency or narcissism.* For males, it's domineering or emasculating behaviour; females can suffer from masculinization or extreme passiveness. In other words, "Your either an asshole or a bitch, or a pushover and doormat." You want to find the sweet spot. Both extremes are antithetical, which depolarize the healthy dominance in a man and the radiance in a woman. I'll explain polarity in great detail in the next chapter. For now, I'll share some examples and the effects of what unbalanced polarity can cause.

## WHAT'S WRONG WITH THIS PICTURE?

Ladies, he plans the first date, picks the time and restaurant and you accept. Then after reading reviews and talking with your friends, you text him back and suggest a different place, because you found one with a higher rating. Another example, you're on a dating app and match with a guy, he asks for your number so he can call, but you say, "No, give me yours I'd rather call you." Both of these experiences have happened to me, and both times, I told these women it wasn't going to work out. Do you know why I wouldn't meet either for a date?

Their *disrespect* instantly turned me off. Why? They judged, insulted and rejected my masculinity. No guy wants an ungracious or controlling woman who isn't willing to receive his leadership. Let alone when she throws it back in his face. It doesn't matter if you think choosing a different restaurant would be better. You denied him the only gift he wanted to give you. You've essentially told him his suggestion wasn't good enough, inadvertently or not. I may sound like I'm being super sensitive, but it's *far from it.* I believe how anyone does *anything* is how they do *everything.* Likewise, disrespect maps over to every single thing in the same way. This isn't any different from how a woman would feel if her hubby bought her a vacuum cleaner or an exercise bike for her birthday. It may be in good faith, but it's *degrading.* All she hears is, "You're fat, and need to clean the house". Disrespect can be very subtle and thus unnoticed, but it is felt regardless."

The woman who didn't want to share her number had her reasons and probably couldn't trust me. Why did she want to be anonymous? Was she cheating, emotionally hurt, or protecting herself? Either way, she was trying to control me and the situation. She wasn't ready to allow a relationship into her life. How could she with a closed heart? She was overly cautious and skeptical, clear signs she wasn't able to receive. I've noticed dating sites are full of emotionally immature and unavailable hopefuls.

Leadership, provision and devotion are the gifts men give to women, *they're given, not taken.* A woman's gift is her ability and willingness to *receive* them. Women are not *entitled* to a man's love or devotion; she's not deserving just because she has a vagina. She earns it through her gratitude and appreciation for what he offers. Whenever a woman takes that ability away from him, she's being disrespectful. When she denies him his need to serve, he no longer feels he has any purpose. Women should never tell men how to act or what to do. Men are just as disrespectful when they violate, reject or take advantage of a women's gifts; her grace, receptivity and vulnerability.

## DISRESPECTING AND EMASCULATING MEN

"Am I supposed to be a prissy and subservient little girl who kisses a man's feet, bows down and serves him? Fuck that, I'm an independent woman. No one tells me what to do, especially guys. Men are responsible for all the problems, *men*struate, *men*opause, *men*tal breakdown, *men*tal illness, *guy*-naecologist and *his*-terectomy."

Sadly, many women have been *done wrong by men.* When men fail her, it forces her into her masculine polarity. This may be great for efficiency, self-protection and survival, but it's tragic for her love life. Masculine men will gravitate to where they're received and will walk away from where they're not. They will *never demand or force* a woman to *receive* him. Contrary to belief, these men can handle strong, independent and opinionated women, but would rather not. *Not worth the effort.*

I often hear women saying they want a *real man,* yet when one shows up, he's judged and shamed for it. As soon as he displays any dominant traits he's accused of being chauvinistic. When she can't control him, he gets blamed for having insecurities. When she disagrees with his point of view, he becomes guilty of mansplaining, or manterrupting her.

"He's not masculine enough and can't handle me. I intimidate him." Ladies, don't confuse his *self-respect with insecurity.* Only *insecure men* will put up with a woman's controlling ways. Why's it his fault if he won't accept her entitlement and lack of respect? Adding insult to injury, most guys will usually give in because they feel blackmailed, shamed and guilty for being too masculine. He'll gaslight himself so he won't be associated with the evil patriarchy or resemble its demonic offspring. He'll cut his balls off and make himself wrong just to prove this, *which he shouldn't have to.* Modern women are turning princes into frogs and then blaming them for it. Don't get me wrong, there are many insecure and overcompensating douchebags out there.

When guys say they want a strong woman, it's because they lack that strength in themselves—*they're emasculated.* Not putting up with a woman's disrespect is not about a lack of confidence, it's because he's turned off. Ladies, if a man pranced up to you wearing a pink dress, painted nails and red lipstick and said, *"OMG, I love your shoes"* would you feel sexually attracted to him? This is the same reason a guy won't feel attracted to a woman who displays masculine behaviour. Like a magnet, attraction is due to polarity—similar energies repel—and opposite ones attract. Strong women repel masculine men and attract emasculated ones. Weak men will attract controlling and strongly opinionated women.

Masculine men won't put up with being disrespected; they'll address it... or leave. Emasculated men will acquiesce, shut off or pull away; they have no power to address or correct it. Strong or weak, every man *will sense* when a woman is dishonouring him. He may not know why or what it is, but he will feel the irritation in his body.

## THE WAYS YOU DISRESPECT MEN

Whenever you force or manipulate a man to adjust his behaviour in any way, you're belittling him. You're implying he's a useless little boy incapable of figuring things out on his own. That's what mothers do, and it's patronizing. Mothering may seem like you're loving and caring and to an emasculated man, it will, but not to a masculine one. You may have the best intentions, but it's *condescending*.

One of the worst injuries you can inflict on a man is disrespecting him. A man doesn't like his independence being challenged, nor his agency questioned. If he is standing in honour, he'll do the right thing to the best of his abilities. When you judge or assume what the reasoning is behind his actions or words, you're emasculating him, and *it's offensive*. He may be full of shit, but before you jump on him, give him the benefit of the doubt. Ask to clarify, he may be right, and you overreacting. Don't make him wrong to make yourself feel better or to avoid being triggered. You have no authority to tell him his intentions are different from what they are.

*You're not to soothe his delicate ego, nor should you expect him to tough it up so you can continue dishonouring him.*

Honour his choices, and then you can share how they make you feel. Whenever you offer a solution, assign a chore or tell a man what to do, you're putting him in a position to resist, or submit to you. *You're leading him, and he feels like you're cutting his balls off.* You may believe setting rules and expectations is empowering, but it's not. You've become a dude and emasculating him in the process. Radiant women never have to do this; they simply need to express their feelings about the situation, then let him serve in the best way he knows how. Never demand or be unwilling to make compromises. Telling him how *he should feel* or what *he should do* will turn him off. If he does submit, it's done against his will; an obligation. He'll feel extorted, especially if he calls you out and you start crying because you don't like it, or know he's right.

Men are wired to give and they won't stop doing so. If you reject him, he'll find someone else who will receive them. Your need for control will break him down. He'll withdraw, especially when you try manipulating him into acting in a certain way. When you resist or try to edit his guidance, you're gaslighting him, he's no longer giving from his agency. Entitled women rarely take accountability for their behaviour and will often degrade a guy's character when he calls her out. It's never her fault because her criticism is always justified; if he stands up to it, he's an asshole. Her emotions are made to be more important than his reasoning, or verifiable proof. When women feel hurt, they'll resort to shaming. They also don't like when they can't play the victim or get the outcome they want. *Men are easier to control when they are feminized.*

**Every time you** don't appreciate, trust or admire him, hold off sex for punishment, assume he isn't sincere and honest with his emotions, don't ask him to do important tasks, hire renovation work without his knowledge, are not interested in his passions and achievements; judge, criticize or complain about him, accuse him of being a child, make him act feminine, are demeaning about his financial status and virility, compare him to others, interrupt him, accuse him of wanting to control you and bringing up the patriarchy card, roll your eyes, make fun of him, are impatient, over nurturing, don't let him help you and do the tasks assigned to him, say he's not good enough for you, talk down to him, don't accept his compliments, say you're a guy and you're all the same; ignore his suggestions, ideas and solutions, judge his actions and criticize his character, give him shit for not loading the dishwasher right, yell at him for accidentally breaking something and every time you challenge or belittle him in front of others especially your children, you're being disrespectful. Lastly, if you've trivialized anything I just said, *you're being ungracious.*

## SHIT TESTING

I get why women initially shit-test guys, because they're interested, and see he's a potential suitor. She wants to make sure he's the real deal and not just a chump before she commits. *"Is he safe enough to trust, and be vulnerable with? Will he protect me and our children?"* The disrespect comes when she doesn't stop testing him after he's proven himself. If he keeps jumping through her hoops, he's a *circus animal or puppy* she can control. If she can puppeteer him, she'll lose her respect and attraction for him. Most guys keep pandering in the hopes of winning her favour. Women will bait a guy simply because she's bored, or because he's not grounded in his masculinity. If she fully trusted him, she wouldn't try to control or set boundaries.

Men need to call this behaviour out from the beginning. If he doesn't, it normalizes and there's no going back. If she continues, he needs to firmly state why he's *choosing* to walk away. Guys, you're responsible if she acts up or gets dramatic; if she does, you've lost your leadership. Men need to *correct* a woman's behaviour if they're violating them. When they do, they're accused of judging and trying to control her.

Judgement gets a bad rap, it's not about name-calling or ridiculing, it's about *discernment*. When a guy judges, he's giving directives; it's for her betterment, a gift to her. When a woman tries to correct a guy, *it's controlling* and shows contempt. So is when she uses her emotions as a weapon to penetrate him. This is a violation of his autonomy, something he shouldn't ever have to defend against. He's there to protect her, not to defend himself.

Setting boundaries is a masculine trait, they are like walls. The more of them a woman has, the more she imprisons her radiance and blocks out her light. When she judges a man for being feminine, she doesn't realize she's in judgment and her masculine polarity. There are so many ways respect can be violated—I can write a whole book on it. I'll touch on two more points before moving on. Guys, if your girl is still hanging out with her single guy friends, *she is poachable.* If she won't stop going out with them after you've made it clear you're not comfortable with it, she's not respecting you. Also, if she wears provocative clothing on outings without you, and tells you to deal with it after you object, she doesn't respect you. She's presenting herself as being *available...* remember, women, are never single.

## MASCULINITY ISN'T TOXIC
## THE ABSENCE OF IT IS

Stop believing masculinity is *toxic*; it's a bullshit narrative. Studies have shown testosterone, surprisingly, increases honesty in men. "I piss standing up, you need to sit down therefore I'm better than you" isn't dominance, it's being a chauvinistic asshole. When describing what a dominant man is, one has to make a distinction between what he's not. Muscles, beards and tattoos don't make a man; a monkey dressed in a suit is still a monkey. These veneers are external compensations, so is being macho. A domineering man is a really camouflaged bully who appears to be dominant. Dominant men consider everyone's needs in addition to their own, because they're not selfish.

Domineering men are unstable, reactive, moody, jealous, easily triggered and need a woman's validation. This type of man is ruled by what comes at him because he's not in control of himself. This makes him unsafe to be around. The domineer actually fears women; her emotions and feelings threaten his own. He will attack, criticize and put her down to defend his inflated yet delicate ego. The tyrant manipulates her for compliance; she feels like she's walking on eggshells around him. Masculinized men are abusive, spiteful, take selfishly and try to control others. They blame, gaslight, create fear and impose ultimatums; *real men don't.* Toxic men are concerned only with what's in it for them, even at others' expense. They'll deny all accountability and shift blame by deflecting and projecting it away from themselves.

A domineering man will get angry and defensive when he's called out or questioned; he'll lose control and attack. These men are all talk and no action, they're constantly making excuses, promising things will change. Whenever he does change, it's temporary and will only last until he wins back the person's trust. He doesn't have healthy boundaries; they'll fluctuate depending on his mood, or whatever the situation is. His motives are ambiguous; he's unable to clarify his position because he doesn't have one. Nor does he have a clear or defined purpose; *he's lost at sea.* He doesn't penetrate with his truth—he rapes with his anger, fear and lies. He's inconsistent with everything, from his emotions to how he conducts himself. He seeks attention and validation; he lies, twists the truth, is repressive, and has a quick trigger. This isn't dominance; *this is toxic masculinity.*

## MASTER MANIPULATOR

A healthy man doesn't downplay your emotions, nor does he try correcting them. He never tells you to stop feeling what you do. A *masculinized* man isn't mature enough to face your emotional depth and how you express it. Instead, he'll blame you for creating drama or being too emotional; and say it's not his problem. Instead of showing compassion and understanding for your feelings, he'll criticize and gaslight you. He'll make you think you're crazy.

Domineering men also fall into the trap of transferring their *mother's inflicted wounds* onto other women. He believes he's leading, when in fact, he's triggered and acts like a tyrant. Masculinized men will manipulate you by using *your vulnerabilities and feelings* against you. They're covering up their insecurities and childhood wounds. *Be careful you're not emoting his trauma and taking it on as your own. This can turn into mothering and the need to fix him.* He believes what's good for him is good for you. No, you're taking on his wounds, and he's controlling you by them. Then, he'll discard you when he can't control you anymore. You'll realize it was never about *love,* but about *control.*

No man has any authority to tell a woman how to *feel* or what's *important* to her. He has to be okay with whichever emotions she's expressing; *she must also honour and fully embody them.* She's not to appease him by trying to edit her feelings. If he can't handle it, that's his shit. There's nothing wrong with you, no matter what emotion arises.

A man's true strength is not to use force and intimidation over a woman, that's too easy. His show of dominance is having the ability to build her trust, so she opens up and feels safe doing so. When she feels this freedom and can be totally vulnerable, she'll stop trying to control him and let him lead. This is a huge risk for her because what she yields to him, he can use to hurt her. Guys, she has the true power... and she knows it. *You only borrow what she decides to give.*

## DISRESPECTING WOMEN

Guys, do you want to lose the toxic masculine label? Then stop, treating her like your mother or an ex who hurt you, feeling superior or better than her, assuming she's stupid and over-emotional, making her doubt her potential, criticizing or making fun of her, denigrating her goals and dreams, not supporting her, getting too sticky and not respecting her time alone or with her friends and family, disrespecting her privacy, not giving her your full and undivided attention, not listening and interrupting her, failing to keep promises, gaslighting her, invaliding her feelings, making her feel unsafe, being ambiguous, keeping secrets, not apologizing, ignoring and disrespecting her boundaries, not paying attention to her needs, lying, giving the silent treatment, using her insecurities and vulnerabilities against her, being sexually rude and inappropriate, being a slob around her, displaying gross habits, objectifying her unless you've mutely agreed to sex play, displaying narcissistic tendencies and checking out other chicks with roving eyes in her presence. In short, put an end to any form of subjugation against her.

## NARCISSISTS

I once interviewed a woman on my podcast; she was a therapist and a survivor of abuse. She coached abused women and was an expert on trauma, empaths and narcissists. The single and most important advice she gave was, "If you're with a narcissist... RUN! *No, if's and's or but's.* Get out of dodge ASAP!" You'll never win them over. I believe the word narcissist is being overused, and many times, it's unsubstantiated. Ironically, those who judge others as being a narcissist, usually fit the description themselves. As the saying goes, "It takes one to know one." Contrary to belief, *it isn't only men who are narcissists.*

Many don't notice the red flags until it's too late. Here are some traits to look out for: they'll love-bomb you at first to hook you in. When they've got you, they'll start tearing you down and will eventually discard you. The moment you muster up the courage to empower yourself, they'll suck you back in. Since your confidence is low, you'll tend to go back because *they're good sometimes.* When they are nice, they provide the validation you need. They won't change no matter how much you try to sympathize with them. If you're constantly attracting these types of people, you're probably an empath, *the Yin to the narcissist's Yang.* You're in a symbiotic relationship, a trauma bond, which benefits the abuser. *Your light attracts moths, and your warmth attracts parasites.* Dealing with a narcissist is bad enough, but it's much more dangerous when you're dealing with a sociopath, or worse... a psychopath.

Many get *narcissists, psychopaths and sociopaths* confused. A psychopath is devoid of all empathy; they never get shaken; they are born like that. They can kill you, then eat your liver with a side of fava beans paired with a nice bottle of Chianti... and their heart rate will never miss a beat. Psychopaths are usually control freaks, sociopaths act like psychos but have *learned it* from a young age. Narcissist and sociopathic behaviour can be the result of a hard upbringing. The lesser of the three evils is the narcissist, but it's best to avoid them all. Narcissism can be described as an unhealthy aspect of the ego; it's all about protecting an image, saving face and looking good. Ego is not a bad thing per se, as we need it to maintain our self-respect and for our desire to shower... *and to wipe our ass.* The ego is a problem when it gets out of hand.

Characteristics of a narcissist are: self-importance, no empathy for others, non-caring, needing excessive attention, entitlement, needing approval and validation, manipulative, controlling, unable to receive feedback or constructive criticism, easily hurt, jealous of others, vindictive, spiteful, immature, addictions, can't admit being wrong and being hyper critical. Their ego is at stake at all times. They need to find meaning through the manipulation of their reality.

Narcissists love any attention, even if it's negative. So if you think calling them out and getting angry will help your cause, you're mistaken; you're still feeding their need for attention. The best way to deal with a narcissist is simply by not engaging. Starve them out, be monotonic and stoic. You can never win by negotiating... *just leave!*

# CHAPTER TWELVE

# POLARITY THE SECRET OF ATTRACTION

## ANCIENT WISDOM

Until this point, I've tackled the obvious causes leading to involuntary bachelors, spinsters and unhappy partnerships. Here, I'll address the core reason why couples lose attraction to each other, have marriage problems, cheat or fall victim to political and toxic narratives; and just about every other problem occurring between a man and a woman. This is all due to *depolarization*. Understanding and embodying masculine and feminine polarity addresses all these concerns. Although I don't believe in *panaceas* per se, polarity correction can be considered such an *elixir*. This isn't a one-and-done-pop-a-pill-quick-fix solution, but something that takes hard work, dedication, commitment, perseverance and undoing years of subconscious programming to achieve. Although simple in theory, healing isn't an easy process. Similarly, losing weight is also an easy concept; eat less crap and exercise more. How many can commit to it?

In the secret teachings of Hermeticism, the philosophy of Egypt and ancient Greece; there are seven spiritual laws. One is the *Law of Correspondence*—patterns repeat throughout the universe—as above so below, as within, so without and so forth. This applies to everything in our reality. Nature is governed by these seven laws and these patterns can be observed within all things animate and inanimate. The other six laws are *mentalism, vibration, rhythm, cause and effect, polarity and gender.* All these principles apply equally and interconnect. My teachings focus primarily on the last two; *polarity and gender.* I'll be using the law of correspondence to explain how everything, is the same as all things.

All of creation is dual, every thing has a *pole* or an *opposite.* The law of gender states; there is *masculine and feminine* energy embodied within all things. No thing (nothing) can be created in the physical, mental or spiritual realms without these principles. Two ancient symbols represent *duality.* and masculine/feminine energy. They are the *Tao and the Six-Pointed Star.* Many are familiar with these symbols, but only a few truly know their meaning.

The six-pointed star is formed by two overlapping triangles; one is pointing up and the other down. Together, in their centre, they create the shape of a hexagram. This symbol is found in the Roman, Hindu, Japanese, Phoenician and Ethiopian cultures, but is mostly recognized as the Jewish Star Of David. The masculine is symbolized as the triangle pointing up towards God, its tip penetrating the Heavens. The feminine is the triangle pointing downwards to Mother Earth, the receiver and the chalice.

The other is the *Yin Yang* symbol depicted in Ancient Chinese Philosophy. The *Yin* and the *Yang* are contained within a circle and represent both positive and negative forces. One half is black and represents the feminine, and is called Yin. The other half is white and represents the masculine, and is called Yang. In each other's half is a dot of the opposing colour. This symbolizes the cycle of nature. It also shows that a portion of the opposite condition is always inherent in the other. The circle itself embodies the oneness of all things.

We have both male and female energies within us, one is at the forefront and the other is integrated into the background. This polarity can be witnessed everywhere, not only in humans but in *nature, spirituality and science.* Duality can be observed by acknowledging the opposing conditions in all things: hot/cold, light/dark, hard/soft, etc. Each extreme is simply *the opposite state of the same thing.* Pain and pleasure vary only on the amount of pressure the masseuse applies. All is one, the difference is only on where a point is measured on the spectrum. Perfect balance or the middle point is neutral and offers no tension. Opposition is what creates friction, or in other words, *attraction.* In this polarized state, there is a pull for resolution and homeostasis. Imagine a teeter-totter or a stretched elastic band.

## SCIENCE

*Magnetism* is the force exerted by magnets when they *attract* or *repel* each other. This force is created by the motion of electric charges. All magnets have two poles; the north pole (negative) and the south pole (positive). *Note: no penguins or reindeer have been harmed during this experiment.* The magnetic force from a magnet flows from the north to the south pole, which creates a field. This produces the law of; *opposite charges attract—like charges repel.*

*Electricity* is energy produced by the flow of electrons. They flow from one point to another. These two points are called electrodes. All batteries have two ends, one is negative and the other positive. The female end is called an *anode* (a negative electrode) and the male end is called a *cathode* (a positive electrode). Electrons flow from negative to positive. *Male and female electrodes are required to make electricity flow.* Our body is such a battery that stores and releases energy. Together, a magnet and an electrical charge form and create an electromagnetic field. That's the buzzing you feel around those you're attracted to.

The human brain has two hemispheres, the *left* and the *right*. The left side is considered *masculine* and controls the right side of the body. This hemisphere is associated with *thought*, logic, reasoning and action; and represents *electricity*. Conversely, the right side is considered *feminine* and controls the left side of the body. This half is equated to *feeling*, intuition, creativity and expression; and is considered *magnetic.* The conscious and subconscious minds also share different polarities. The conscious is masculine and represents the mind and brain. The subconscious is associated with the heart and the body.

In sacred geometry, *lines* are considered masculine and *curves* feminine. Men have lines and women have curves—*the circle and square.* Adam's rib is the *line* used to create Eve. Man creates the structure for the woman to fill. Imagine a colouring book, the empty lines are waiting to be filled with colour. Men create the container and hold the vision, and women fill it with love, intuition, grace, multicoloured feelings and expressions. She animates and brings everything to life; *literally.*

Without structure, the image seen in the kaleidoscope would be just a blob of muddled pigment and so would the wings of a monarch butterfly. Man is the stem that supports the rose flower and the oyster that protects the pearl.

## SALSA BELLA

I was always fascinated by salsa dancing. The Latin American culture embraces sensuality and romantic expression without inhibitions or taboos. In the 1960s, Puerto Rican and Cuban immigrants distilled this sexual chemistry and instilled it into the magical dance form called *Salsa.* The Salsero stands in an erect pose, powerful and majestic like a matador in the bullring. He possesses precision, speed and control—his Salsera, postures in an elegant stance at his bow. He moves and leads her... *and she follows willingly.* This represents the *authority* inherent in the masculine and the *surrender* in the feminine. He is her anchor that supports her movements. She submits to where he moves her; this allows her the freedom to embellish and express her deepest impulses. During the entire time, she never leads or challenges him. When a man can lead a woman, it gives her the safety and trust she needs to express herself in absolute fullness. Life is a Divine romance; leading and following maps over to everything in the human dance of love and attraction.

I believe salsa dancing should be used for marriage counselling. A woman I once dated taught salsa dancing. She knew when there was trouble in a couple's marriage just by observing them, as they danced together. Wife to husband, "You're not doing it right. Stop screwing it up." Teacher to wife, "No, he's fine; *you're the problem.* Stop trying to lead and control him." As soon as the wife allowed her husband to lead and *stand in his masculine,* over time, not only did their dancing improve but also their marriage.

Unlike English, many languages around the world are *gendered.* They contain masculine, feminine, and to a lesser extent, asexual or neuter characteristics. Latin and all its dialects, aka the romantic languages, such as Italian, Spanish and French, are gendered. Interestingly, they're considered the languages of love and seduction. In Italian, *Bella* is used when referring to the feminine, and *Bello* is for the masculine. All nouns are gendered, and each depending on the sex, influences how we see them. They directly affect our cognition, especially our feelings about the opposite sex.

For example, in Italian, the word used for a key is, *La chiavetta,* which is *feminine.* The adjectives used to describe it are *small, shiny and lovely.* In German, the word used for a key is *Schlüssel,* which is *masculine.* The attributes used to describe it are *hard, jagged and metal.* To non-Germans, Germanic must sound very harsh. Being of Italian descent, I can affirm swearing in Italian is much more potent and satisfying than it is in English.

## MASCULINE & FEMININE TRAITS

**MASCULINE:** Yang, directive, penis, sword, penetrate, impales, thrust, jab, ejaculate, sow seeds/sperm, farmer, external, logical, think, lead, strong, devote, dominate, action, find solutions, judge, fix, protectors, ensure safety, survival, logic, reason, action, firm, survival, loyal, adventurous, competitive, rational, strength, confidence, inner strength, responsibility, focus, decisive, stability, clarity, boundaries, courage, discipline, capable, certain, assertive, goal orientated, needs a purpose. Straight lines, I think, external, produce and put forth.

SYMBOLIZES: fire, expansion, light, hot, intellect, sun, hard, etc.

WIRED TO: to lead, serve and protect the feminine; hunter.

SHADOW: domineering, perpetrator, abuse of power, unstable, aggression, controlling, confrontational, criticism, abuse and avoidance.

POLARITY KILLER: being criticized, controlled and subdued.


FEMININE: Yin, expressive, vagina, cups, receive, hold, carry, incubates, absorb, nurture, fertile soil, grow, receive the seed, internal, chalice, womb, intuition, healing, gentle, wise, patient, feelings, flexible, creates, cooperative, radiates, emotions, soft, submissive, follow, unconditional love, understanding, nurturing, tenderness, kindness, intuitive, creative, collaborative, flow, radiance, surrender, sensitivity, emotional, ease, allowing. Circles and curves, I feel, internal, consume and take in.

SYMBOLIZES: water, contraction, dark, cold, intuition, moon, soft, etc.

WIRED TO: follow, receive and share with the masculine; gatherer.

SHADOW: controlling, manipulation, victim, powerless, weakness, withholding, neediness, codependency, over-sensitivity and over-emotional.

POLARITY KILLER: feeling unseen, unsafe and misunderstood.

## WATER AND FIRE

When a woman is acting *Yang*, she's in her *masculine fire;* she loses her water. Man loses his fire through the extinguishing element of *Yin, feminine water*—he loses his erection and her vagina dries up. *The sexual attraction is dead.* One cannot receive when they are in their masculine energy, nor can they penetrate when in their feminine, *regardless of gender.* Without water, she can't receive him; without fire, he cannot penetrate her—*viagra and lube to the rescue.* Without water, she cannot birth life or express her passions and creativity. Water represents emotion, tears and feelings. Weak men lacking fire are not only impotent in the bedroom, but also in their relationships, and every aspect of their life. He needs to penetrate with his truth, purpose and leadership—all pervasively. Like water, women are *slow* to boil; like fire, men are *quick* to arouse. Men need *fire* to get a woman's *water* boiling.

Guys, if a woman doesn't appear feminine to you, it's either because your masculine energy is weaker than hers, or she's become masculinized. Ladies, similarly, if a man doesn't appear masculine enough to you, it's either because your masculine energy is stronger, or he's become feminized. Regardless of gender, when one polarity is strong, the other will change to compensate. Nature is always trying to find its balance. Men who are attracted to masculine women embody more feminine energy—women attracted to feminine men embody more masculine energy. Have you noticed *dominant* women are usually with *passive* male partners?

A man can polarize a masculinized woman back into her feminine if he's strong enough in his masculine pole. She will soften, but it won't be easy. He has to figure out if it's worth his time and effort to do so, especially if she has deep emotional wounds. Have you ever encountered a healthy relationship where both couples were *dominant, or submissive?* This is rare, but if it happens, it's a snoozefest... or a war zone, a battle to determine who submits first. Dominant women fare better with submissive men and vice versa.

Feminine women with an integrated masculine are more attractive to masculine men who have their feminine equally integrated. Likewise, these women are attracted to men in their masculine polarity, those who have a properly integrated feminine energy. Notice how this balance is depicted in the Yin Yang symbol? He needs feminine energy *(feelings)* for his moral compass; she needs masculine energy *(discernment)* for her zeal. This harmonization leads to respecting, trusting and following the inner wisdom within ourselves. We have both aspects inside us, but until we've evolved spiritually, we need the opposite polarity embodied in another to help us integrate it.

A balanced woman is graceful, yet can assert herself when needed. In turn, the integrated man is direct, yet can empathize with a woman's emotions. The conscious mind has to trust the intuition of the subconscious mind. One has to follow their heart, but sometimes our desires can lead us astray and override our logic. We need our masculine and feminine energies balanced and integrated.

## CAN POLARITY BE FLUID?

I've been asked for my views on polarity in homosexual relationships. I can't answer authentically, because I'm not gay. I believe these types of partnerships are more complicated due to the involvement of similar genders. Unless each partner has an assigned and fixed role, there will be a fluctuating power struggle. In any successful relationship, there's always the one who's more dominant than the other. Having said that, *polarity* is only possible with *equality*. This means neither leadership nor submission is inferior or superior to one another. An Oscar is awarded to both the lead and supporting actors.

Can polarity be fluid? Some believe this works depending on the situation and we adapt when the need arises. Roles change depending on who's better at a task. Others will argue polarity has no sliding scale. Like a switch, it's either on or off; it attracts or repels. Some contest it's more like a dimmer switch. Let's look at science again to satisfy this argument. When an atom has an equal number of electrons and protons (negative and positive charges), its total electrical charge is *zero*. Which means, the atom is *neutral*. Conversely, if an electrician is careless and touches two hot wires together, the line shorts out it and blows the fuse. The light stops working because there's no longer energy flowing to it.

In the law of duality, opposite poles are static; the closer you get to the middle of the scale, the less attraction there is. Unless one has mastered the ability to jump from one polarity to the other or can turn masculine and feminine energy on or off at will, there may be a chance for them to experience fluid polarity. Sadly, most can't even stay in one pole with enough consistency to fully embody it.

Many will pose the argument that there are a lot of gender-fluid animals in nature; such as the bearded dragon, clownfish, wrasse fish, banana slug, whiptail lizard, cuttlefish, parrot fish, garter snake, blackfin goby, cardinals, butterflies, green turtles and frogs. Clownfish are all born male and when needed, the dominant ones will turn female. Some species of animals can take on the attributes and duties of the opposite gender. Male seahorses, for example, are the ones who get pregnant and give birth to their offspring. Female hyenas can display a pseudo penis by protruding their clitoris up to ninety percent the size of a male. Since ducks and geese are known to rape their females, evolution has afforded them the ability to create decoy vaginas. These artificial sacs are used to prevent penetration and divert sperm from going down the wrong path.

This is all fine and dandy, but... we aren't *animals*. This argument doesn't hold up. We would've evolved like them if we were meant to. We are enslaved to our hormones. Sexual identity may be fluid in one's *mental* and *emotional* state of being, but *not in one's body*. Humans have fixed gender traits. Unless, of course, they're altered artificially by surgery and hormone replacement therapy.

## DEPOLARIZED INVERTED AND UNBALANCED

*Depolarization* occurs when one or both charges *(masculine or feminine)* are reduced, or neutralized. *Inversion* happens when these poles flip, or change to their opposite states. *Unbalanced* energy is when there's too much of one polarity without the counterbalancing effect of the other. *Depolarized, reversed and biased* states of polarity are harmful to our mental, emotional and physical health and well-being. Unless our energies are fully grounded and integrated, we will fluctuate between masculine and feminine energy, due to hormones, past conditioning, stress levels and circumstance. Healthy polarity has the dominant pole at the forefront, and the secondary pole residing in the background. Without the counterbalancing influence of their opposite charge, these polarities can become *excessive.*

All things must be in balance, always and in all ways. The equilibrium of duality has to be maintained, *as in the tension between the two.* Chaos ensues when they become untethered, as they keep the other in check. If not, one or both poles becomes despotic and will cause havoc. The governing homeostatic effect prevents either pole from indulging in its extreme tendency. Masculine and feminine energies rebalance excessiveness. Many farmers will tell you when hens are displaying erratic behaviour, the presence of a cock will calm them.

When masculine energy becomes excessive or lopsided, it can lead to an uncontrolled and destructive force. Men left on their own without feminine energy to rebalance them can cause problems; like carelessness and loss of perspective on what's important. Men are naturally goal driven, but when they have blinders on, they can develop tunnel vision and become overly competitive—they'll focus on a single goal and nothing else matters. They can become domineering; this is due to the lack of feminine empathy present. This can be considered *toxic patriarchy.*

Women are governed more by emotional signals than logical ones. Generally, they care, feel, suffer and fear more than men do. *This makes them more sensitive and anxious.* Too much feminine energy can overrun her emotions and can cause erratic behaviour. She'll be more susceptible to external influences. Men perceive this behaviour as neurotic and will call women irrational and full of drama. Emotions are a woman's way of interpreting and communicating, as thinking is for a man. This doesn't mean she doesn't think or he doesn't feel. Obviously, we utilize both, but when men *feel too much* and women *think too much,* it creates an unbalance.

## WHAT CAUSES INVERSION

Many factors can cause or influence inversion. We live in a world where our food, water and personal care products are loaded with dangerous chemicals, like endocrine and hormone disrupters. We have stressful jobs and living conditions, which raise cortisol and invert our body's estrogen and testosterone levels. Infuse that with the engineered social narratives, gender politics, trauma and everything I've covered so far, further distorts and homogenizes gender roles and polarity. We've deviated away from natural law. This has created so much divide and confusion.

How do we know what constitutes healthy polarity when our perception of masculine and feminine energy has been distorted? Men confuse femininity based on appearance and women misinterpret masculinity as alpha males and domineering narcissists. We may appear masculine or feminine, but most of us are just hiding behind our toxic representations. We will fawn over and appease these facades in the hopes of redeeming ourselves. The *answer is* not found by fighting harder, or by pandering; these approaches are futile. The solution is to correct our imbalanced and inverted poles.

Polarity is the result of having healed and integrated our masculine and feminine aspects. We can't blame the world for our depolarization, nor should we seek remedy solely through our partners. We're responsible for fixing it. Thankfully, our partners can help us. Why else do you think we're attracted to them?

Seeking a partner while anima or animus possessed, will attract similiar counterparts; those who we will further damage by our own imbalance.

# CHAPTER THIRTEEN

# CREATING POLARITY

## AWAKENING

Polarity is the red pill that will unplug you from the depolarized relationship matrix. It's time to polarize and create some electrifying and epic sexual attraction. This is no easy feat, especially if you've had years or even decades of inverted programming. Undoing depolarization doesn't happen overnight; it takes commitment, effort and constant recalibrating. You may not even want to re-polarize yourself, maybe you're happy with how things are. If you're a dominant woman, or an emasculated man and happy with the status quo and making it work, awesome! We all have free will and the right to choose however we want to live and with whom. Who am I to judge? But if you're reading this, it's obvious you aren't happy with how things are. Your biology has probably caught up with you and is pushing you to take a deeper look at your current situation.

To create polarity in your relationship, first, you need to polarize yourself, then you'll need to heal the dynamics with your partner. Let's look at how we can integrate our masculine and feminine energies so we can experience polarity within ourselves and in our relationships. We need to know what it means to be a dominant man and a radiant woman—*true masculine and feminine embodiments.*

## MASCULINE DOMINANCE

Many people mistake *dominance* for *domineering*; there's a distinct yet subtle difference. Just as there is between a guy who's *cocky* and *confident*, in *control* or *controlling* and one who's *emotional,* versus one who's able to *feel emotion* without drowning in a pool of his tears. There are also healthy and unhealthy aspects of dominance. Most people associate dominance with being an Alpha male. Being this type of man doesn't automatically ensure an integrated or healthy masculine persona. In truth, many Alphas are often conceited, selfish and don't truly care about others. I was discussing *dominance* at a party with a female friend, she thought I was referring to guys who took longer to get ready than women, or those who spent hours admiring themselves in front of a mirror.

Similarly, there's a difference between having *power* and being *forceful.* Power attracts naturally; force is coercive and manipulating. A dominant man never postures or pretends to be an Alpha; not once does he try to convince anyone, especially women. He knows himself and doesn't have to prove anything. Dominant men don't take from others for their gain, because they have principles, and integrity, and are less concerned about power, prestige, position and pesos.

Integrated men don't brag, or flash their cash or their car; if they do, they're most likely overcompensating for the real thing. These types of men are insecure, attention and approval-seeking bullies who are afraid of being called out. Being dominant doesn't mean pile-driving weaker men into the ground, or banging women hard against a wall. This isn't to say some don't want a wild n' rough fuck every so often. Patriarchy bashers should aim their crosshairs at domineering men, not at healthy masculine men.

## CAPTAIN OF HIS SHIP

Dominant men are leaders and will serve others before themselves. They'll be the first to apologize and make sacrifices for the greater good. They'll go down with the ship and protect women and children first, then their fellow man. He'll take another's needs into account in addition to his own; this means being selfless and doing the right thing no matter what. As a leader, he'll accept all liability, even if he breaks his own rules—he knows he's not above his own standards. He admits when he's wrong, he's protective and in servitude. He knows where he's going, what he wants and what his purpose is with clarity. His word is sacred, yet he still honours his desires. Dominant men embrace their masculinity despite all the anti-patriarchal narratives. He's not afraid to lead, nor threatened by *chauvinistic* and *sexist* name-calling. Neither is he guilted into submitting or gaslighted by the misogynist guillotine looming over his head.

A dominant man is led by his *purpose* and his *truth*, not by his feelings (*his emotions guide him, they don't control*). He's established strong boundaries and won't easily be swayed—not even by a woman's fluctuating moods. If her mutable emotions can throw him off, she'll lose her attraction for him. She wants a man to take control as a caption does his ship. Her high winds and swaying moods must not take him off course or puncture holes in the hull of his boat. Dominant men know where they're going and are consistent and reliable. They aren't affected by what comes at them; their skin is thick and they don't take anything personally. If the world can have its way with him, so can she… and that's a turn-off for her. She wants a captain with a dash of pirate added, one who is wise enough to utilize her emotions as a compass, to navigate through life. This is why a man's emotions need to be anchored and integrated before she's willing to set sail with him.

A dominant man still feels fear but will break through it regardless. He has honour, integrity, and morals; he doesn't bend when pressure is applied. He's unmoving like a tree with strong roots, yet yields to the wind, but never breaking. He never controls, forces or imposes, he simply leads; his confidence demands that she follow. His confidence is evident and his purpose is a priority. His truth is penetrating, consistent and reliable. He's always striving to rise to his magnificence. A man who is dominant takes ownership of his emotions, actions and reactions. He will not blame anyone but himself. A dominant man is never jealous; he's confident and independent. He governs what arises from within and knows the outside has no power.

A dominant man will praise and encourage his woman, never for approval, but for her benefit. His devotion is selfless, yet he is penetrating. He affords her safety, security and trust through his *attention and care.* He takes responsibility for his actions, but doesn't let her transfer her emotional responsibility onto him. He provides a protective container for her to feel safe enough to express herself, and to take accountability—so *she can process* her emotions.

The dominant man treats his woman like his Queen; he will serve and protect her heart at all costs. A man is never to domineer or control his woman like a tyrant King because *this isn't dominance—it's cowardice.* He knows her well-being is his responsibility; he respects and honours her needs. Guys, you can't fake any of this; she'll smell it immediately. Work on yourself, be the man she wants and truly desires.

## LEAD HER

One of the challenges of being a high-value man is picking the wrong woman. Due to his high demand, he's got many options to choose from. Unlike beta males, who can only pick from the discounted leftover rack. Confident men don't settle on whoever likes them; they decide on who will enhance their life. A dominant man can walk away from any woman who doesn't value or respect him. The feminized man needs to stick around because he's needy and afraid of losing what he has—he regularly puts up with her disrespect.

Guys, you'll need to be strong, or you'll be drawn in and lulled by her beauty. You'll be like a crack addict and feed off her radiance. Be careful not to become sexually or emotionally dependent on her; *oxytocin addiction is real.* Drug dealers usually treat their buyers with contempt; addicts lose their rational thinking and will do anything to get high. Once you rehabilitate, you may be surprised at how unattractive she can be; regardless of how hot she is, or great the sex is. Your *lack of boundaries and self-control* will allow her to wander recklessly into emotional chaos. She'll be unable to control herself and will start running the show. Why? Because it's in her nature to do so. You'll need to take control and drive, or she'll take the wheel.

Don't do everything she wants, call her out on her shit and don't react to her tests. Never defend or justify yourself; she's only looking for a boundary. A woman should be a compliment to your life, not your total focus. You're a man with a mission who's not easily swayed. Don't always agree with her, or buckle when she shows resistance. You succeed by not taking the bait, or letting her lead you. Never let her pussy or her moods compromise your principles, or your mission. *Even if she's your soulmate, never act out in fear of losing her.*

Don't change for her; she fell for you as you were. If you allow her to change you, you'll lose her. If she needs you to change, *she isn't the one.* If you're single, don't chase women, work on yourself and create your empire first. The right one will show up when you're ready, not when you're pretending to be. You can't force anyone to follow your leadership, especially if you're bad at it. Lead, if she doesn't follow, be prepared to walk away. You're a rarity, a high-value guy who has options. Remember, she'll want you more when she knows other women want you. She wants to be your prize, the one you desired the most—the one you chose out of the multitudes clamouring for you. When you find your purpose and know where you are going, *you'll be in high demand.* As a high-value man, you'll never need to sell yourself, because women are already standing in line, ready to buy. You can thank her biology for that. *Know thyself* first, then be clear on what you want.

Women are influenced more by their emotions than by facts, regardless of how apparent they are. They are the *masters of feelings*, you'll lose if you try to fight fire with fire. Your woman will grind you down, but you need to stand firm. Challenge her and let her prove you wrong, not by her feelings, but by rationale. "Babe, there's a difference between needing a purse and wanting a Louie Vuitton. Our budget is tight and you don't need a five-carat diamond ring or a royal-styled wedding." You're the captain and you set the terms of your ship.

*Caution: there's a time and place to lead.* You're not to micromanage her life. She also has autonomy and a right to her terms. If it's not in your wheelhouse, let her choose for herself. You're not a tyrant, nor ruler over her life. You don't get to tell her what brand of makeup is best for her. This doesn't mean you can't tell her how you'd like her to wear it. You do have authority over things that affect both of you; things like life insurance and major life decisions—this is where you lead. However, *you must take her feelings and concerns into account first*, then come to a decision... *together*. Eventually, you'll learn to anticipate her needs even before she has to ask. At times she may not understand what you're doing for her and she'll resist, but do it anyway. She'll love you for it later.

## OWN HER

We both know who wields the true power, and it's not the guy. Women have what men want, and they know it. If she's clean-shaven, her bra and panties match, she chose to have sex, not you. All forms of penetration are possible because she lets it happen, otherwise it's a violation. Men have a physical advantage, but it should never be used coercively, or violently to domineer any woman. He has autonomy, and so does she. No one rules over anyone.

Men only borrow the power women hand over to them; it's a *privilege*, not a right. Men have to earn a woman's trust before they'll give it up. Once they do, they can't take this responsibility lightly, not even for one second. Guys, you need to be in total devotion and keep her safe; her well-being is in your hands. When she submits, she's saying, "I trust you to lead, keep me safe and help ease my burdens. You are the captain of our *relation-ship*, and I have faith in you."

Even though women want safe and honourable, they also desire the billionaire vampire. So become that character in their fantasy. Be the one who objectifies her, controls her body for your pleasure and does whatever you please with it. You need to trigger her primal sexual energy and be the man she wants to submit to. Let her know you're a sexual being, and sex is important to you. This doesn't mean it's all you talk about. Don't be a pig or a try-hard who forces it on her.

In the early stages of dating, bring sex up subtly, but don't dwell on it. Just plant the seed and move on. Touch her often and know when you reach her threshold; before she reacts or tells you to stop. You need to anticipate her needs and boundaries at all times. If she says you're too touchy or won't show compliance, she isn't ready yet, or willing to submit. You'll need to build more comfort and trust. If all that doesn't work, she isn't for you. You want to get to the point where you can grab her hair by the nape, pull her head back, bite her neck, or kiss her without any resistance. Not because you *forced* it, but because *she wants it.*

She wants to be desired but reserves the right to withdraw consent at any time. Treating her body as if you own it means doing what you want to it, whenever you want. *Caution: doing so always within pre-agreed limits and with a safe word.* If a guy is attuned to her, she'll never need to say it. Sometimes, she desires a low-empathic guy who doesn't need permission to devour her. He has to be dominant in a healthy way. She's taking a risk by going all in; she must be able to trust her assessment of you. Her life is in your hands, emotionally and physically.

Women *want men* to be in control of their life. They won't hand over their power if they're not trustworthy. You need to be transparent, authentic, congruent, self-aware, patient and observant *of her* and her surroundings. This means being mindful of her feelings and every subtle response she displays. Create the safety and space she needs that allows her to trust you and let her guard down. Your strength will make her soften, become vulnerable and be open to receive you. *Never toy with her; this is serious business.*

## FAT JEANS & DINNER

"Babe, do I look fat in these jeans?" Do you lie not hurt her feelings, or do you tell her the truth? However you answer it will be wrong because it's a trap, but only for a feminized male. Tell her the truth, she may not like it, but she'll respect you for it. Although, it's wise not to be an open book, *never lie to her and never be mean.* Even if that means it'll hurt her for that moment, she'll trust you more when you're honest. *"Babe, since you asked, those jeans make your ass look fat. You know I love your butt, so try on another pair. These will look better on you."* When you tell her how you like her to dress and keep reminding her of how hot she is, there's no room for her insecurity. Telling her what to wear makes life easier for both of you. *She'll want to look hot for you.* Also, being honest shows her you're in control and not affected by her changing emotional states.

Self-respect and total confidence are essential to be worthy of a woman's submission. Lesser men will *act as if* they have it together; they'll use false bravado and a cocky attitude to ruse women into believing they're *the man.* Then will freak out and attack when it doesn't work, which it never does. Confident men are happier and have more to give than insecure ones. Posers are selfish and feel disempowered; they take instead of giving. They'll try to control everything and everyone because they lack the confidence and resources confident men have.

Set the bar high and hold yourself to these standards. Own your mistakes and don't be afraid to admit when you're wrong. A dominant man isn't threatened by failure or appearing weak. He can take rejection and will welcome a challenge. Everything is a gift or an opportunity to learn and get stronger. Only weaker men are afraid of admitting to their mistakes. Wearing a mask to hide behind keeps us on guard and in fear, because it may come off and expose us, and shatter the facade.

Where do you fall on the *chauvinistic/chivalrous* scale? There's a fine line these days. Chivalry can be offensive to some modernized women. They can interpret *opening a door for them* to be patronizing. I used to believe in dating equality, like going dutch on first dates and letting her decide what she wanted to eat. Why wouldn't I want to give her what she wanted? That's when I was emasculated; *polarity actually triggered me.*

A Russian woman once told me, "Men have to pay for dinner because we spend lots of money to look beautiful for you." I immediately thought she was a materialistic gold digger. She may or may not have been; I couldn't know it then. Nowadays, I'll arrange the date, choose the restaurant and pay for dinner. I'll even find out what she likes beforehand and order it for her. But, if my Russian friend didn't put in any time or effort into looking good for me, or if there was no potential ROI (Return On Investment) even after the second date, it was a definite "Net (no)." I'd move on and let her know I was dating other women. I wasn't going to invest until she showed me she was willing to herself.

Eventually, I got tired of buying women dinner or paying for those who made a sport of getting free meals. I resorted to going for coffee or walks, instead of investing in her. This was safe and lighter on my wallet, but it had no emotional impact. It showed I was a cheap beta male who was afraid to invest and lead. I learned to evaluate a woman's potential before investing, however, *it will always be a gamble.* Guys, you can't get mad at women for using you, especially when you let them.

In the past, I'd cringe at thinking like this, let alone write a book on it. I've learned to hold my frame and realize others, especially women, are guests in my reality. I'm sailing the ship, if you're onboard, you're my passenger. If you don't like where I'm going, you can jump, or take the dingy back to shore. *Have a nice day, "Ciao ciao."* I've stopped trying to impress women on first dates. *I quit being the dancing monkey vying for her attention.*

Masculine men are rare and have a higher value than regular chumps. Modern guys want women to lead because they're weak pussies afraid of getting rejected. They wait until it's safe to ask for her number; they hope she'll offer it. They'll ask permission to kiss her and apologize the second she shows any opposition. Guys, grow some balls and learn to deal with her resistance. Stop letting the feminist movement hold you hostage and guilt you from being a man.

## FEMININE RADIANCE

Do you know why men love women in high heels? Most will say it's because it makes her legs look longer and raises her butt *thirty percent* higher. This mimics *lordosis*, a posture where a woman's lower back is arched downwards to expose her bum, indicating she is ready for sex. This may be so, but I believe it's because high heels make a woman appear more vulnerable. I once saw a video where a woman was kicking the shit out of a boxing bag, MMA style, then later dribbling a basketball wearing the same stripper heels. She looked stunning but I didn't feel any attraction to her whatsoever. I'd much rather have seen her walk delicately in those shoes. Seeing a woman walk and striving not to wobble is sexy. Men respond to that; whether it activates lust or his protector instinct, it's the vulnerability that makes women *feminine.*

A radiant woman carries the sweet and soft innocence of a little girl—definitely not the immature side. She moves and speaks with grace. She's grateful for what her man offers through his devotion and accepts his leadership; this is his gift to her. In return, she gives him her gift; her willingness to receive him, her trust in his leadership and her desire to express herself vulnerably from her heart, without any manipulation. *This is how both thrive.*

Seduction is a masculine trait, as it holds an outcome. This includes using the eyes to penetrate and lure men in. Are you the type of woman who reveals a bit of cleavage or one who exposes three-quarters of her boob and a hint of areola? Do you dress *hot* to seduce or because it makes you feel good? Believe me, I'm far from being a prude. Women need to understand one approach attracts unhealthy predators and the other, healthy and protective men. There's a difference between flirting and cock teasing. Although still considered sketchy to some, burlesque has an innocence to it. This art form is far classier than a vagina rammed three inches from a guy's face taunting him into handing over his money. Might as well point a gun at him.

Femininity is *expressing* beauty just for the sake of it; there is *no motive. A bee is naturally drawn to a flower, it's attracted by its grace, colour and fragrance.* Some plants, like the Venus Flytrap, also have flowers, but come with a serious caveat—a hinged carnivorous trap. Masculinized women are like such a plant and often eat unsuspecting visitors. They attack and penetrate with their words, actions and expectations, which are masculine traits.

Femininity is a woman's *superpower.* There's a difference between a *feminine woman* walking into a room versus one that *just looks like one.* A graceful woman governs by her heart and feels safe residing there. She's present in her body and trusts its messaging—she isn't ruled by her head, obsessive thinking or trying to micro-manage every situation. A feminine woman owns her feelings and doesn't project or blame anyone else for causing them. She has self-respect, knows her boundaries and when to walk away from a non-devoted man. Such a woman doesn't waste her time or energy trying to change or fix men. She doesn't try to teach boys to become men nor treat them as such. She knows when a guy is authentically devoted. She'll soften and can open up and receive him... *but only when* she knows he values her.

She can detach from her past experiences and see them as lessons without blame or needing to protect herself. She's soft, gentle, permissive and radiant. This doesn't mean she's a wallflower or a doormat. She won't wait for the man to change, nor be forced to ride on his selfish crazy train. She knows how to express her needs in a way he will respond.

## DOES HE NEED TO STEP UP FOR YOU?

Do you wish your guy would step it up, rise to the occasion and be a real man? Many of you do, but have you ever considered your behaviour may be the reason he isn't? He could very well be a man-child incapable of being the guy you want. Maybe you are aware of your behaviour and how he's responding, or you don't and are wrongfully blaming him for everything. Are you in your feminine radiance and is your heart open and soft? Are you disrespectful, entitled and not responsible for your feelings and actions? Do you underestimate or condemn him in any way? How do you react if he screws up, like breaking a plate while unloading the dishwasher? Are you on him for trivial things? You say you admire him... but even after he does or says stupid things?

No one is perfect, we're all *wabi-sabi* (yes, go look that up). Men are waiting to rise and willing to serve you. They will and do in proportional response to the depth you surrender to their leadership. Sadly, they're not given the opportunity. Men are only inspired to act when they find the solution through their leadership, which they acknowledge from your vulnerable feminine communication. He interprets your every command as an attack and disrespect to his autonomy. This kills his desire to serve you. *Ladies, you need to learn this.*

There's a difference between *allowing* and *offering* no resistance. Allowing your man to do something is still trying to control him. *"Mommy, am I allowed to have some ice cream?"* Letting someone do something sounds like they need to ask for permission or register for a permit. You don't allow a man to be dominant; he is or he isn't. If he is, you submit to his leadership, or you don't. I once heard a man say, *"I'm the boss of this house, but only with my wife's permission."*

Men are attracted to and inspired by radiant, heart-centred and emotionally vulnerable women. If you only knew how powerful you are, how a pure heart can make any man fall to his knees. You'd know he would do anything for you, a far cry from him sitting on the couch and ignoring your bitching. Why would a bee go to a flower if it didn't have any fragrance or pollen? Why would a man be drawn to a closed-off, critical, defensive and unemotional woman? The same reason why they won't respond to childishness, victimhood, manipulation, emotional blackmail or anything forcing or implying them to do something against their will. Men need to be inspired, not dictated to. *Your judgements don't inspire him, your feelings do.*

## DON'T MOTHER HIM

Women believe they have to take care of their man and anticipate his needs. No, that's what mothers do for their sons.

Only moms direct, teach, set boundaries and expectations. If a man lets his woman mother him in any way to please her, or if he lets her buy him clothes, he's emasculated. *Mothering is extremely depolarizing.*

Stop giving him back rubs when he isn't leading you to do it, he'll ask you if he wants one. If you want to give him a massage, you'll need to ask him for permission. Giving him anything unsolicited, whether it's advice or your opinion is leading. This behaviour is masculine, and it will turn him off. It's simple, if he doesn't lead you to do it... *don't.* Sure, nurturing him may be great at first because he'll feel loved and spoiled, but then he'll get lazy and needy *and you guessed it—bye-bye attraction.* If you're giving to get something in return or because you feel insecure, you're grasping; it's manipulation. As bad as mothering him is, so is acting like a demanding spoilt child.

If he needs sex, you must oblige, *but only* if you feel up to it. He has to be aware of your needs; if you're sick, feeling bloated, or on your menses. If he isn't considering how you're feeling and is still demanding it, he's a controlling and selfish asshole. If he wants morning sex and you need a bowel movement, let him know. Don't flat-out reject him or hold out because you want to punish him for something he did last week. If *you want sex,* he will know. You can verbalize it and say, "I feel horny babe." and "Can I give you a blowjob?" Women can also be selfish regarding sex and believe men are *always on,* and they'll never say no. Sometimes, he's also tired, stressed or not in the mood. Funny how women can turn down sex, but men can't. *A guy has to be understanding,* but she's allowed to tear a strip off him if he refuses... *hey, men get headaches too.*

You cannot mould a dominant man into being what you want him to be. You're not a sculptor or his mother, no matter how much you try convincing yourself that he needs your guidance. The emasculated guy will twist into a pretzel to please you; *boring*. The guy you truly want will command you to go deeper, or he'll leave. You're worthy of him and all he does for you; there's no need to manipulate or beg him to do anything. Your self-worth is all it takes to make him want to devote to you and so does your ability to receive what he's offering.

## DEAR MEN & WOMEN

When a woman receives a man, *she lights up.* He feels appreciated and will ramp up his devotion; this also makes him *feel amazing. The more she receives him, the more he wants to give her.* This creates a feedback loop and builds a magnetic field which keeps expanding—it feels good for a woman to be in her feminine and for a man to be in his masculine. The more freedom he feels in the relationship, the more he'll devote to it. Have you noticed the more you do for a man the less he will do for you in return? *He's the doer and you are the receiver.*

Man's greatest need is to *lead* and to be *received* by his woman. She wants to be cherished and feel protected. If he's not *penetrating her,* she can't *receive him.* Likewise, if she isn't open, he can't penetrate her. Ladies, the more you emasculate him to fulfil your needs, the more he will shut off. You'll be stuck with a beta-servant-sycophant-slave. He'll cheat on you or leave, and because you can't respect him either, you may do the same. Being a doormat is just as bad as his emasculated behaviour.

Many will challenge me and call me a misogynist, "Frank thinks women should be passive wallflowers. He believes women shouldn't have any choice or a say in anything." Umm, no...it's the furthest thing from the truth. Ultimately, in courtship, the woman is the one who *chooses* and the man is who *decides*. In *chapter fifteen,* I explain how vulnerability is a woman's superpower; she actually has the advantage.

You've learned the characteristics of polarity and how it's created. Now what? How are you going to interact with your partner? You'll need to learn how to properly communicate with them.

# CHAPTER FOURTEEN

# COMMUNICATION

## DO YOU UNDERSTAND
## OR INNERSTAND?

When you were a baby, the only way you knew how to communicate and express your needs was to cry; until you learned how to speak. Many have a bachelor's degree in English and still don't know how to communicate properly. You can swear at someone in a different language and they may even laugh because words carry no weight unless they're received. Nonetheless, *the hardest language to speak is the truth.*

Words are preloaded, each carries a charge and land differently for everyone. What triggers one person is funny to another. *Cunt* is such a word, I don't know many women who aren't offended by it. The meaning a word carries can also vary, for example, *"Take the fags from the casket I've put in the boot."* If you're English, you know what I tried to say. "Take the pack of cigarettes I've put in the jewelry box from the trunk." If you're from North America, you're probably thinking I've got a bunch of dead homosexuals in a boot, which I'm bringing to the cemetery. Identical words can have different meanings, even between adjacent villages located on opposite sides of the river.

"Actions speak louder than words" is an overused but true aphorism. "Talk is cheap" is also cliched and abandoned advice. Words comprise only about *seven percent* of human communication, the rest is non-verbal; *intention and body language.* It's not *what is said, but how it's said, or what isn't*—also, the tone is very important. To communicate *effectively,* three elements need to be in alignment; *what you think, feel, and say.* These affect what *we do;* the holy trinity.

Unless you're dating a psychic, understand, your partner isn't a mind reader and won't always know what *you mean.* You have to be clear with your *words and intentions.* Over time, you'll learn to anticipate what your partner is saying, and even what they want before they even mention it. Those who aren't self-aware, are prone to betray their instincts and will rely only on the words they hear. Speech alone can camouflage *ninety-three percent of* non-verbal expression, which can be used to deceive or manipulate.

## WTF JUST HAPPENED?

Men attach importance to what is being said, and take words at *face value;* women are concerned more with the *emotional impact* they impart. It's not what a guy says, it's how it makes her feel. Women have a less direct way of communicating, unless, of course, they are in full-blown attack mode. This can lead to conflict, and it took me a while to figure it out. I was on a road trip driving with a girlfriend; she asked me if I was hungry. I thought, *"Wow, she really cares about me."* I wasn't hungry, so I answered "No." We both smiled at each other, and I continued driving. Thirty minutes later, out of the blue, she exploded in rage. We got into a heated argument for no apparent reason… *there's always a reason…* I'm like, *"WTF just happened?"*

When she asked me if I was hungry, what she was really asking was, "Are you hungry, because I sure am. So I suggest you find us a place to *eat right now.* My blood sugar level has dropped to bitch mode… *I need food.* I'm going to search my memory for the last time you didn't listen to me. Ah yes, three months ago, you were an asshole, which I'm still pissed off about. You're a selfish bastard and never consider what I need." *"WTF? Why didn't you just fucking say so?"* Believe me, I've learned from that experience. Ever since, I always keep a snack packed away in the glove box of the car. So, the next time your woman unexpectedly explodes on you, here's what you do. When she erupts, give her wine and some chocolate… and proceed with caution.

You may be thinking, "Wouldn't it be so much easier if women just said what they wanted instead of having us decode complex riddles?" You either learn a woman's code, *which is a losing battle because she'll change it on you without notice,* or lead her into expressing how she's feeling. But if she tells you what she wants directly, that would be leading, and you don't want that either. What guys don't grasp, is that *womanese* is a language influenced by emotion and less by rationale. She's literally speaking a foreign language. Guys like to fix problems and will offer solutions; women tend to share how they feel about them. I've also learned when your girl opens up to you, don't try to fix anything, at least not right away. *Trust me on this guys.*

Most people don't want to be *fixed;* they just want to be *heard.* Listen to her first, be fully present and offer no remedies. When she's done talking, ask her, "Do you need me to listen, or do you want me to offer a solution? Often, they just needed to purge, and sometimes that's enough. You'll look like a miracle worker, and you haven't done a damn thing. *You're welcome.* Sometimes, women complain because they're just emoting their feelings and nothing more. She may not want any advice at all; maybe she just wants a hug or an ear to listen. At times, she may not even know what the problem is, and just wants to feel bad. This drives a guy nuts because it doesn't make any sense to him, nor should it. *Ce la vie.*

Leading her to use feminine communication removes the need to decode her. Relationship coaches seem to miss the mark on this one. Many are *depolarized* themselves and have no clue how to properly communicate in their own relationships. What they teach are distortions. They teach women how to *empower* themselves and men how to gush out their *feelings.* They're not aware of polarity; this is causing more problems than it's fixing. Women shouldn't be directive when communicating with men because it's masculine behaviour. Likewise, men shouldn't be sharing their feelings with women, because it's feminine be-haviour. I'm not saying men should be stoic, just less effusive.

## HEARING AND LISTENING

Communication means engaging in a *dialogue,* not a *mono-logue.* I grew up in a household where everyone interrupted each other. No one listened to what anyone said; they only waited until someone stopped talking so they could get their three cents in. I remember suffering anxiety because I needed to speak quickly; I was afraid of being cut off, which I often was. I never felt *heard,* nobody did; this left me feeling invali-dated. Everyone talked over each other, and it only got louder and louder. People who don't feel heard, go silent or get defensive. They begin to argue and push their views even harder. *Then everyone stops listening.* In high school, the rockers and rappers would blare their music and try to overpower each other's tunes. At that point, it was just noise and became *a war of the decibels.*

When speaking about important matters or during a ceremony, the Indigenous peoples often use a talking stick or feather. Whoever holds it has the right to speak uninterrupted, others could listen but not comment, unless asked. This created a safe environment where everyone could be heard. I know families that pass a spoon around in place of a feather. Being Italian, we also had a spoon, it was made of wood and was used much differently. When it was shown, we listened!

Men hear but they don't always listen; they can be selective and will catch what's important to them. Women will hear words guys didn't even say, or would even think of saying. When it gets to this point, communication is lost and turns into a yelling match. Guys will shut down and begin to ignore everything he's told. All he hears is Charlie Brown's teacher muffling, "Wah wah woh wah wah." This drives women nuts and will make them nag and bitch even more. She loses her shit as he sits lifeless on the couch.

When communicating with your partner or *with anyone,* make an effort to understand them. Speak with clarity and try to see their point of view. Are your words landing properly? Do you wait until they've completely anchored before proceeding? We need to be specific and may have to reiterate what we mean.

Don't *assume* the other person knows what you're talking about. "You know what I meant." *"No... I don't."*

Many are familiar with *unconditional love*, but only a few recognize *unconditional understanding*. This means getting out of the way and listening non-reactively; slowing down and feeling how your words are impacting those you're talking to. *To be understood, you need to understand first.* We often get ahead of ourselves, become impatient and sometimes condescending; we may resort to manipulation to get our points across. You can communicate all you want, but if it's not grasped, it's like talking to a wall.

There are many ways to aid and clarify your communication. You can say things like, *"Yes, I said that already, but maybe you didn't hear me. I know what it means to me, but it may not mean the same to you. What does that mean to you? This is what I heard; is this what you meant? I don't recall; we remember things differently. If you continue speaking to me like this, I'm stepping away from this conversation. I have my truth, and you have yours, I'm not debating any further. Yes, I hear you, and that's not my experience."* We have to put ourselves in the other person's shoes and be open to their views. We may not be seeing the whole picture.

What someone says or how they behave towards you shouldn't ever be taken personally, nor considered an attack. Unless you choose to accept something, it isn't yours. If a blind person calls you ugly and you believe them, who's the fool? Our ego often takes what others say and makes it personal. It creates an imagined story about itself and attaches an identity to it. The avatar is what's being triggered, not you. Our ego will attack and defend against anything threatening its existence. What is it defending, *ideas and memories?* None of them are real. *We are not the ego; not everything is about us.* When someone throws shade on you, it's never about you. It's about their insecurities and fears, which they try to project onto you. *Don't take the bait.*

## THE BODY TALKS

*Listen to your body.* Some believe our brains are in control of everything. Some follow their heart regardless of what their mind says. Throughout history, songs, poems and plays have been written about this internal struggle; *the heart vs mind.* There's little mention of our other brain, *the gut.* Did you know we have three brains? There is the three-pound grey matter we carry in our head, our heart and our gut *(lower vital parts).* The *brain, heart and gut* all have intelligence. Some believe our brain is just a puppet master sorting files in a mailroom. The *heart* senses the world through feelings and emotions; the *gut* is how we understand the world and our identity in it. They say, "Trust your gut" for a reason; it's our intuition and the instinctual feelings we get when we know something feels off.

Did you know the heart radiates an electrical field *sixty times greater* than the brain and is *one hundred times* stronger? The field it generates lies *several feet* outside of the body. The heart's magnetic field not only receives and processes our feelings, but also affects other people's moods, attitudes and feelings. Masculine energy is associated with *thought and thinking; the mind.* Feminine energy is associated with *emotion and feeling; the heart.* The merging of *knowledge* (masculine) and *understanding* (feminine) gives birth to *wisdom* (child). Knowledge is all the available information—understanding is based on that information—and wisdom is what's done with that information.

*Thought* plus *emotion* equals *action; knowledge* plus *understanding* equals *wisdom.*

So what am I getting at here? When our energy fields are resonating and are in *congruence,* the body is in *harmony,* grounded, feels good and is energetically *strong.* When it's in *dissonance,* irritation is felt, and the energy field *weakens. All three brains need to be in sync.* Not many people have developed the awareness to notice these signals. If they are, they're often bypassed and at the least, misunderstood. During stress, women pop out of their bodies and bring their awareness up into their heads. They go from a feeling and sensory-based state to an over-analyzing and neurotic one.

Men do the opposite when they're stressed; they get too deep into their emotions and lose their *objectivity.* A flood of emotions will consume men, and avoiding them will cause women to get lost in the chaos of their thoughts. This depolarization is immediately felt in the body as *anxiety and irritation.* Polarization on the other hand, feels good. When we don't feel safe, our body and three brains will tell us something is off, *"Mayday, mayday, we're lost, we've strayed into foreign territory!"* A polarized partner will help us get back into balance, into homeostasis and bring us back home.

Our body is always communicating with us. We're constantly receiving and transmitting information with others, hormonally and energetically. Trust your feelings and instincts, always and in all ways. If you've noticed, your gut always ends up being right. Instinct or truth is known in the body, not in the mind. The challenge with communication occurring between men and women is due to their varying characteristics. We feel, think and experience different sensations in our bodies. Women can't feel the cringing in a man's body when he's spoken to disrespectfully; they can't understand his internal resistance to it. This is a reason why female relationship coaches shouldn't be coaching men. Likewise, guys can't sense a woman's emotional depth, fear and uneasiness when she feels unsafe; but he can use his reasoning to lead her out of the storm without getting lost in it with her.

## EMOTIONS

Emotions are neither *good nor bad;* they're simply feedback or information. It's the story we build around them. Emotions are bad only when they're denied, judged, and used as weapons. Ignored feelings become stronger, fester and covertly rule the subconscious, which affects our behaviour. Behind all physical and emotional pain is an *ignored feeling.* There it sits and waits, hiding until out of nowhere, like mentos in a coke bottle it *violently explodes.* Slowly, and over time, perpetual outbursts begin to erode our delicate nervous system. Deep neurological grooves are formed and they become the only path available when we get triggered—we slide down it like we're on a luge track. We're often held hostage and addicted to the rush it gives us, like a junkie wanting more drugs.

Fire can destroy, or transform. Anger and frustration can crush us, or they can propel us forward to make positive changes in our life. Sadness can help us pay attention to the details we may be overlooking. Pessimism can help us prepare for any potential obstacles that may arise. Feeling guilt can help upgrade our moral compass. Anxiety can help us solve problems. Jealousy can be a motivator and make us work harder, and so on. The challenge is knowing if your jealousy is about caring, control, dependency, fear or lack of trust. It's *normal* to react with jealousy if you've been cheated on, and it makes you wary in a new relationship. What isn't, is if it makes you constantly worry about and wrongfully accuse your partner of cheating. Then you'll start blaming yourself for driving them away and continue going deeper into the chaotic storm.

Whether they cause you to *smile, cry or explode in anger,* we can agree *emotions are powerful!*

Horses are very empathic creatures; they can feel well beyond our ability. They also don't take what they sense personally. This is why they're used to treat those suffering from trauma and mental health issues. Horses mirror back what they feel without judgment, so the sufferer knows what to address within themselves. When horses face any threat, they remove themselves from it; until they feel safe and no longer in danger. Then as if nothing has happened, they return to grazing. They don't build stories, join chat groups, or analyze the event as we would. Since we aren't horses, we need to learn strategies or seek out others who can help us. Many spiritual gurus teach us to be in the present moment and to disassociate from the *past and future.* Focusing on the past brings *sadness, regret and depression* and *worrying* about the future, stirs up *fear and anxiety.*

Ladies, your emotions whether you perceive them to be good or bad are *your gift to a man.* They show him how you feel and what you need. *Never be ashamed of them.* When he knows how you feel, he can better serve you. The best way to *communicate* with men and have them *respond positively* is by expressing your emotions *vulnerably.* If you don't feel safe doing so, you'll try to protect yourself and attempt to control the situation. You may get triggered into a fight or flight response, and the anxiety will consume you. Rational thinking goes out the window, heightened self-criticism, self-doubt, negativity and obsessiveness fly right back in. These are unconscious and uncontrollable attempts at trying to manage a trigger response. Feel your emotions, but don't allow them to overwhelm you.

## A WOMAN'S FEELINGS MATTER

Unfortunately, many women feel their feelings don't matter. They do and are *extremely valuable;* they're the most beautiful thing. Not only are a woman's emotions her gift to men, but also the world. When she's not radiating or unable to express her feelings, she suffers... everyone does. Ladies, your feelings are worthy, they're your value—there's no need to justify them. Repeat these words, *"I have value and am worthy, simply because I feel."*

Your vulnerability is a man's inspiration; he's attracted to your *ability to feel and express yourself.* When you know your worth, you'll unapologetically move away from any man or situation who doesn't value you. If he doesn't respect and protect your heart, if he takes advantage of your vulnerability... *walk away,* your not a doormat. You're not a pin cushion for unsolicited penetration. Conversely, he should walk away from you, if you're constantly disrespecting him. *Soften...* he can't penetrate you if you have a chastity belt on. I'm not referring to your female bits exclusively, but the armour protecting your heart. He doesn't want to keep breaking his dick trying to penetrate Fort Knox.

Masculine men want feminine women who can express themselves. Hiding your feelings attracts weak men who can't handle the full spectrum of your emotions. Concealing your emotions is another way of controlling an outcome; it's masculine. Self-respect means you won't dim your light to protect yourself. You'll shine bright for those who can see and cherish you... *all of you.*

Being vulnerable isn't about being unsafe, it's about feeling safe to express yourself. Yes, it's a risk and scary to be vulnerable. Your goal is to express your feelings only; it's not to make anyone else happy. Your grace is never conditional on an emotion, *every feeling is worthy,* but they need to be fully expressed. There's no need to pawn them off. Own them without blaming anyone and bring your awareness deep into what you're feeling. *Can you be a witness and just observe your feelings?* Express it vulnerably without trying to control anything—without seeking sympathy or playing victim. You'll only spiral deeper into shame and guilt, and it will dig you into a deeper hole.

You're not responsible for anyone's reaction or inability to witness your *all-ness*—but you're fully liable for creating undue drama. When you're in your authentic state, it's not to appease anyone. No one or man has any authority over how you feel. Never stifle your feelings. If it feels like you're walking on eggshells around a guy, it's because he's emotionally immature. Submitting to avoid his backlash isn't submission, you're being bullied and you're placating him. A woman never surrenders to abuse; she yields only to herself and her vulnerable heart.

Being happy when the sun is shining is easy; storms reveal a person's true character. An integrated man will see your anger and sadness as passing clouds temporarily covering your shine. If he needs you to stay perpetually happy to prove your radiance, he's got some more work to do and probably has mommy issues. Take full responsibility for all your feelings regardless of what they are. It doesn't make you wrong or unworthy, but it will to a domineering man-child.

## BATTEN DOWN THE HATCHES

When a man is saturated in feelings, he loses his *discernment*, when a woman is in judgment, she cannot *feel*. A man needs to have his feminine aspect integrated; he needs to know how she feels without being overrun by her emotions. When she's emotionally responsible and can fully express herself, it gives him the ability to lead, provide and protect her. Emotional responsibility doesn't mean suppressing or controlling your emotions; it's letting them out whether you believe them to be good or bad—not deflecting or blaming anyone for causing them.

A woman's feelings act as a compass, which helps a man navigate and guide her. His leadership is the boat, and her emotions are the weather; he has to adjust the sails and control the helm to get to the desired destination. Emotional regulation is important for women to learn, and men can help by providing the container. However, if his vessel isn't sound and he's also emotionally unregulated, they will both drown.

An integrated man is a true knight in shining armour; one who saves the damsel in dis-stress. He's not the white knight simp, but a man who steers her back into her body. *Only a hero not held captive by his emotions can guide her out of her emotional storm; out of her head and back into her heart.* Likewise, only a Queen can lead her King out of his destructive chaos and coax him back into his purpose. She does this through her radiance, compassion and caring heart. When the storm comes, both have unique strengths that will help each other through.

**Quick exercise:** when an emotion does take you hostage, take in a deep breath, relax and become aware of your body... feel your feet on the ground... allow your awareness to drop deeper... scan your body without judging... when you've identified the feeling, notice where it's sitting, allow it to unfold... expand it, and feel into it further. Keep breathing deeply relaxing the body; this will give you more clarity. Without editing or building a story around it, observe what message you receive. It will be the first you get, not the mental banter afterwards... disassociate by looking at it objectively. When you get the message, thank your body and let it go.

Guys, if you're going to help her through the storm, listen to her intently, understand and validate her feelings. Don't disagree or judge how she feels because it's not about you. You don't have to be understood or need to make her yield to your point. Never tell her not to feel what she's feeling. You are dishonouring her when you say, "Don't be sad." She's allowed to be... also... to hate you at that moment.

# CHAPTER FIFTEEN

# MASCULINE & FEMININE COMMUNICATION

## REJECTION

We're born with two basic fears; the fear of *falling* and loud *noises*. The rest have been learned, which our subconscious uses to keep us safe. *Rejection* is something both men and women have learned to fear. Although acquired, it stems from an intrinsic need to survive. Men are afraid to be *rejected* and women fear losing the power *to reject*. For guys, it's approach anxiety and the fear of being turned down. In tribal days, if a woman said *no* to his advances to court her, his value would plummet and it would leave him potentially alone to die; his lineage would end. Women fear losing the power to say no, whether it's by their inability to protect themselves against assault, or by no longer having sexual influence over a man. *Women are afraid of not being desired.* The fear of rejection affects our ability to effectively communicate—primarily with the opposite sex.

The initial stages of using masculine and feminine communication will be uncomfortable; vulnerability is scary shit. Attempting *to lead is scary for men, as* is *for women to let go of control.* No one wants to be vulnerable or lay their heart on the line. Women fear getting judged for expressing their feelings; they don't want to appear weak. Men are afraid of the criticism and resistance they may face if they try to lead. They also fear being labelled toxic and controlling if they try to take charge. If you can't rip the band-aid off and endure some pain, you'll never be able to communicate effectively with your lover. You'll forever be protecting your pride and delicate ego.

Women fear the possibility of being overpowered if they were to stop resisting or controlling; they also don't want to have their emotions used against them. If a man *is* domineering, a woman should be concerned. This is why she needs to listen to her body when it tells her it isn't safe to open up. Guys are also concerned about being manipulated by her emotions; they're afraid she may exploit his devotion. Unless he's hopelessly unaware, he can also sense when his body is signalling caution. When he's not afraid to lead, his leadership *will thrive—* when she feels safe to open up and receive, her radiance *will bloom.*

## MASCULINE COMMUNICATION

To properly communicate with your woman, you need to take the lead and learn three important things; how to: *Discern, Direct, and Elicit* (DDE). Your job is to ask her how she feels, and from her response, you need to guide her back into her feminine polarity. This takes discernment or corrective judgment; *not to be mistaken as criticism.* Your goal is to direct her to take responsibility for her emotions, and make her feel safe enough to express them *vulnerably.* She'll trust your guidance, or she won't. If she isn't receiving your direction, it's because she doesn't trust or respect you enough; you'll need to earn it.

Until she's convinced on a visceral level you're trustworthy, *you are not... so be patient.* You can continue impressing her until you've proven your honour, or cut bait if she isn't receptive. Only you know if she's worth the effort; due to her past, she may be unable to trust anyone. Attempting this should never be done through your ego. Your devotion, provision and protection *need to be selfless.* They are your gifts to her, not for you to feel smug about yourself.

Your goal is to get her out of her *head,* and grounded back into her *heart/body.* You'll need to be fully integrated with yourself beforehand, or you won't be able to help ground her. This will be a challenge, especially if she's used to overthinking and assuming control. Reread the section on *Weathering The Storm,* because you'll be opening Pandora's Box. All her wounds and traumas will resurface and attack you. If you don't know what you're doing, you may re-traumatize her and damage yourself in the process. She'll be too afraid to open up, will resist and close off even more to protect herself. You need to be strong and able to subdue her backlash.

Don't let her project away from her heart and into blame. Make her feel safe, keep her on the course, hold her responsible and in the heart of what she's feeling. Corrective discernment needs empathy, firmness and patience. Remember, *it's not about you,* you're doing this for her betterment. If you can't catch her, don't push... she'll fall. If you're an asshole or incapable of holding the container, don't attempt this because you'll further damage her.

There's a difference between *how she feels and what she thinks.* She may believe she's being vulnerable, when actually, she's just lost in her head and overthinking. You'll have to lead her out of this dichotomy. At first, she may not know the difference because she's so used to being in her head. She may think what she perceives corporally are *feelings,* when in fact they're only *perceptions.* When she begins to express how she feels, you'll need to help her clarify and distill those feelings down to their core. This needs to be done gently and by asking more questions. You'll need to squeeze the lemon until all the juice is gone. "What's under that feeling? What other feeling does it make way to?" When you finally lead her into the nucleus of a feeling, ask her what made her feel that way.

If she says, *"I feel betrayed."* She isn't expressing a feeling but rather a judgment. Betrayal isn't an emotion, it's an act done against someone. The real question is, "What are the emotions you feel as a result of that action. Are you *angry, sad, fearful, surprised, disgusted, insecure or confused* about what happened? "Why do you feel betrayed?" *"I'm angry because you broke a promise."* Ok, she's angry, now you know why. Her *anger* may be the emotional reaction underneath her feelings of *unworthiness,* being *unheard* and feeling *insecure.* You may get generalizations at first, which you'll need to unpack. She may also go on and say, *"Nobody loves me. I always get hurt,"* etc. You'll need to clarify and ask, "Do you always get hurt? Nobody has ever loved you?" Lead her away from, *"You made me feel this"* to *"This is how I feel."* If you're at fault, then you need to adjust your behaviour.

The more masculine she has become *(due to her need for self-protection),* the greater she'll try to deflect her responsibility for how she feels.

Feelings need very few words to be defined, at times only one is enough. Thinking and analyzing can go on forever, so be aware of this mental trap; a psychological labyrinth. You'll also need to avoid her emotional vomit without getting caught in your own shit tornado. Don't blame her for her drama, it's your lack of leadership that lets it happen. If she's going *crazy,* you've lost control, not her. Those in a triggered state, lose their critical thinking. The brakes in the car have failed, and the gas pedal is stuck to the metal. As a consequence, *never tell a woman to relax,* or expect to have a rational conversation at that moment. Don't gaslight her because you don't know what else to do, or can't deal with her outburst. Also, don't over-communicate or emote because you'll get caught in the storm. She needs your composure, don't play the victim or share your feelings. This puts even more pressure on her. *She doesn't want to hear your problems; she needs your solution.* You have two ears and one mouth—*listen* twice as much as you *talk.*

## PENETRATION

Rape is not only committed physically, it's also done emotionally and energetically. Guys, you have to penetrate her with your words and behaviour cleanly. This means without domineering, harming or violating her in any way. Respect and care are traits of masculine men. Penetration cannot occur with a limp dick; this applies to every interaction you have with women. Softening your words, or remaining silent in fear of her potential backlash makes you impotent. If you act like a turtle at the first sign of resistance or rejection, it's no different than your dick shrivelling back into its pubic shell.

Are her words too cold? Are your balls climbing up into your stomach where it's nice and warm? If you can't handle her emotional storm, you aren't man enough to lead her out of it. Stop dancing around issues by non-direct and passive communication—*that's feminine speak.*

When communicating, never use the word *please*, it sounds like a question. This gives her authority over you and forces her to decide your fate. You lose your agency. The one exception to saying please is when using it in a dominant tone, "Please stop disrespecting me." By doing so, you're letting her lead and be in control. I know rejection sucks and you want her to feel safe, but man up and take charge. You give women authority each time you give them your number in the hopes they will call you. *You need to ask for their number, with no exceptions.* I don't mean to ask as in seeking permission. Never say, "Can I have your number?" That question puts her in control of the outcome which is again, masculine behaviour. Remember, she has the power to say no, and you need to honour that… always. If you want her number, simply say, "Hey, I think you're awesome and I wanna hang out. What's your number?" She'll give it to you, or she won't.

Asking a woman for permission is like serving your balls to her on a silver platter. This will make her pussy dry up like sand in the Sahara desert. She may not even know why she suddenly lost attraction for you, but her body will. The is the same when asking if you can kiss her; *don't.* Dracula doesn't ask if he's allowed to bite; she simply surrenders to him. She'll show you via body language if she wants it or not. If she does, you'll know. I caution you, never force yourself on a woman. If you do so it's rape, and you should be locked up in jail alongside a cellmate who calls himself Daddy. Penetration, whether it's emotional, energetic or physical, *needs to be consensual.* Know her boundaries and respect them.

Unless you're into kinky sex play, would you want a woman wearing a strap-on to penetrate you? No? So why do you let her peg you with her words and behaviour? If she does, you'll need to stop it immediately. Direct her by saying, "Stop, this is disrespectful. I'm not having it." Don't ask, "Can you please stop?"

Guys, if your woman is constantly complaining about the same problem, you'll need to step in and correct it; but if it's because of your behaviour... *change it pronto!* If it's not, lead her into expressing what the problem is and *how it makes her feel.* Pay attention to your non-verbal communication; you're responsible for all your actions. Listen to her completely and be as transparent as possible. Give her the benefit of the doubt, be accountable and follow through. When you know you're wrong, admit it. If she's just unloading, encourage her to save it for her girlfriends, or her simp boy-friend. You are her man, not her dear Abby.

Lastly, *discernment and criticism are different.* One is *constructive* and benefits both of you, the other is *destructive.* You don't say, "You're controlling me" because then you're criticizing. A cleaner penetration would be, "You're leading me right now" and explain why. You set the boundaries and expectations of how you want to be treated, not her. Don't let her decide or put that burden on her. Don't be cocky about it, it's about self-respect and *knowing your value and worth*. If you don't convey high value or dominance, she'll lose respect for you. She will eat you alive, then spit you out before breakfast.

*To penetrate is masculine. To receive is feminine.*

## ENGAGE BITCH MODE

You and your guy have finished dinner and you're tired after a long day of work. He leaves the table with plates still on it, goes to the fridge cracks open a beer, sits on the couch and turns on the TV. The sink is full of dishes and you're thinking WTF? You have to finish up a report for work tomorrow and there are two loads of laundry that still need to be done. You work full-time and do all the housework; you feel unimportant, undervalued and taken advantage of. *"If he really cared about me, he'd help me. It's his mother's fault, she let him get away with this."* You want to rip his head off, but you bite your tongue because you don't want to fight and become the nagging bitch. Deep down you know if you complain, you'll make it worse. You've asked nicely before and have managed to control your emotions, for the most part…

You try your hardest not to say anything, but to no avail; you explode! *"How can you sit on the couch when the fucking sink is full of dishes. I've worked all day, I'm tired too!"* You hate yourself because you've become the evil nagging bitch… again. He just wants to chill for a bit after his long and stressful day. For him, the dishes can wait till later, no big deal. For you, it's a slap in the face. A big fight ensues and all hell breaks loose. So how do you handle this in a way that he'll respond positively?

For a man to do anything, he needs to be allowed to do so freely. He wants to serve you, but only if you're not trying to control him; doing so will turn him off. This doesn't mean he doesn't care or is afraid of being told what to do, he's simply lost his inspiration. You've got to understand men; *we love taking care of you and we need to be needed.* We'll do anything for you, but only because we want to, not because you tell us. Yes, sometimes we need a reminder; *we're not all mind readers.* We want to be your hero and solve all your problems.

Smart women know this and will indulge a man, even if they know more than he does on a topic or situation. She'll appear oblivious, let him *mansplain* and finish without correcting or cutting him off. She knows if she does this right he'll be eating out of her hand like a puppy. Guys are typically the clueless ones, some get it though. I don't see anything wrong with not letting on unless, of course, she is being manipulative.

## FEMININE COMMUNICATION

I understand you've had enough and have been hurt in the past. I know you have been taken advantage of for being too nice, loving, patient and understanding. I also believe your heart and trust have been broken *and you have my compassion.* You've exhausted every option and nothing else has worked. You need to protect yourself and take control. You've become jaded and turned into a bitch. You yell and complain because you don't know what else to do. Deep down you know you're making things worse, but you can't help it. So what can you do?

*You need to open your heart;* it's your radiance and vulnerability that will inspire a man to devote himself to you. Men are like a light switch, *vulnerability* turns them on—*blaming* and *controlling* shuts them off. You may accuse him of being self-ish and uncaring of your feelings, but are you truly expressing them? Unless he's a narcissist or a sociopath, he does care for you. You're just not speaking his language, and you're getting mad at him for not understanding.

The hard and fast rule to communicate in a feminine way is to, *never do or say anything for an outcome.* Never *judge or belittle* him because whenever you nag, you're seeking a result. You're directing him, that's masculine communication. To express vulnerably, all you need to do is to *reveal your feelings, needs and whatever the problem is.* FNP (Feelings Needs and Problems). Asking for help is also expressing your needs. Yes, that's it. Sounds simple, doesn't it? In theory, it is, practically... not so much. You may be thinking, *"If I know what has to be done, why can't I just tell him? Is he that stupid he doesn't get it or can't figure it out?"* No, he simply has different priorities and it has nothing to do with how much he cares about you. This doesn't mean you have to be a doormat or passive wallflower either; you just need a different approach.

Guys don't want to be told what to do, most times they don't even know what to do. If the roof isn't caving in, for him, all is well. Expressing your needs vulnerably will inspire him to serve you; yelling or correcting him won't. You have the advantage here, a secret weapon. Your emotions will show him what's wrong and he will respond. So express the problem—never the solution, doing so without blaming, shaming or complaining.

You could say, *"Babe, the sink is full again. I feel sad. I'm over-whelmed just looking at all those dishes. I still have so much work to do before I have to go to bed".* You don't say, *"Hey, empty the sink, I'm sick of doing all the work around here."* One will inspire his inner hero and the other will make him feel like a useless little boy.

You need to express your feelings *clearly and vulnerably,* don't manipulate him or his perception. *He needs to feel how you feel, unbiased and without feeling guilted or blamed.* Doing so will distort and influence his discernment. This is why you want a man whose feminine polarity has been integrated, so he can *feel just enough* to pull you out without getting caught in your emotive net. A man will feel blackmailed when you cry and play the victim.

Women tend to avoid the responsibility of owning their emotions; they'll redirect and blame their guy instead. She'll accuse him of being weak if he can't take it. When he senses this, he'll withdraw or gaslight himself into believing his feelings are wrong. He will feel he's not strong enough and believes he has failed her. The spiritual movement mistakenly teaches men they need to hold space for a woman's emotional outbursts. This is somewhat true; what he needs to do, is to create a container for her to process her emotions safely, not to become her psychological toilet.

Instead of judging him on what *you perceive,* share your vulnerable feelings that were triggered by that perception. You need to take responsibility for your emotions; he doesn't want to be blamed for how you feel, nor should he be. When you say, *"You make me feel angry"* you're putting the onus on him. *He's not responsible for your anger, or misinterpretation of his words or actions.* That's on you; a guy is only responsible for his actions and intentions. If you blame him for the emotions you're feeling, he'll stop listening to you. When you're projecting how you feel onto him, you're deflecting your responsibility to feel them; take accountability.

Sometimes, he won't appear receptive to you, and unlike women, men tend to shut down when they attempt to solve a problem. If they can't resolve the issue by addressing it head-on, they'll retreat into solitude until they do. Women take this personally and will accuse them of not caring. Guys typically don't want to talk it out and share as women do. Give him time and let him figure it out, don't undermine him. Men feel disrespected and pull away when their independence is threatened.

## MANIPULATION & MASCULINIZED COMMUNICATION

There will be a tendency for you to soften masculine communication and believe it's feminine. If it's *controlling, manipulative or directive* in any way, it's masculine. Saying something nicely that is directive, is still leading him; you're just putting sugar on a bitter pill. You're energetically manipulating him into serving you. You may say in the sweetest voice, *"Babe, can you empty the sink please?"* Even if you're subtle, hinting is still telling him what to do. *"Oh look, those dishes are still in the sink, maybe it needs to be emptied."* When you guide him with the solution to a problem, you're not inspiring his devotion, you're emasculating him. He'll feel something is off and not even know why. Or, he may know exactly why and this will aggravate him; he'll feel blackmailed. Why? Because if he resists, he looks like an asshole.

He loves you and wants to make you happy, so he'll his cut balls off to please you. Guys will gaslight themselves and go against their instincts. Sweet talk is sneaky and manipulative because it flies under both of your radars. Your kind words give him no substantial reason *not to submit to you*. If you were a bitch about it, he'd have good reason to resist. Using words like, *"I would really love"* and *"Can you?"* are leading. You're just softening commands to make it appear feminine. You're directing him to do something and he's forced to give in to you. He has no other options because you've already offered him the solution. You're just putting lube on a dildo before you peg him. Even if he's not a pussy-ass-kissing-simp who needs approvable, he'll feel pressured to comply. A truly masculine man won't let you get away with it.

Another way to extort him is by saying, *"If you loved me you'd do..."* You're making him responsible for how you feel. You may convince yourself you want a man who yields to you, but eventually, you'll resent him for it. Your kindness will only produce an increasingly compliant child. Any sense of attraction and desire for sex with him will wane, *and you won't even why.* You may think these examples are petty, but you're slowly eroding his masculinity. You won't have his *devotion*, you'll only have his *servitude*. Secretly, you want him to resist and you probably won't like it—initially that is. You'll thank him later because he's in fact, doing you both a favour.

Other ways you may fall into masculine communication and believe it's feminine is by disassociating from your feelings. Saying, *"It feels like"* isn't delving into what you're feeling, it's another perception. You're not sharing your feelings in a vulnerable way, you're observing and judging them. Using the "I" statement is vulnerable and allows you to express yourself from an internal perspective, instead of projecting outwards.

Beware of another insidious trap which looks like feminine communication but isn't. *"Can I" is correct, "Can we" implies an outcome or an intention.* This is still leading because you're speaking for him. I know this sounds extreme and like I'm splitting hairs, but I'm nipping the problem in the bud. It only takes one cell to cause a malignant tumour.

Become a flower and express your femininity because it's inside you. Just for that fact and for no reason. Why do flowers radiate and exude a pleasing fragrance? Why do they display their beauty? Aside from being for bees and ecological reasons, it's simply because it brings pleasure and joy to the beholder. There is no motive or outcome behind this. Flowers don't compete or hustle, *they are just being.* Feminine energy is an expression of beauty, art, love and creativity. Masculine energy is the opposite, it has a purpose and seeks resolution and outcomes. To paint the canvas and sculpt the clay is a feminine expression; selling it for money or recognition has a purpose and is a masculine trait.

## FEMININITY ISN'T A WEAKNESS

Women are taught it's weak to be feminine, *"To be soft and show vulnerability shows low self-worth and a lack of self-respect."* This BS narrative also implies women are weak when they're not in control. So does complaining and criticizing show women are strong? *Even more hogwash.* Femininity is your true *superpower* and masculine men will agree. Feminists cry, *"If you're not tough, you'll be ridiculed, judged and rejected. Being soft and graceful is the reason the patriarchy oppresses and suppresses you."* Feminists are convinced being feminine will undo all the work their movement has done thus far.

Masculinized women have contempt for femininity and call it sexist. They're triggered because they're in their masculine pole and believe vulnerability will leave them at risk of being dominated in a bad way. This way of thinking is dangerous and is a self-fulfilling prophecy. This inverted mindset is perverting our instincts. If you feel being feminine is weak, you're in judgment and that's a masculine trait. The need to be strong and independent *is a weakness.* Does this offend you? Hold my beer...

Before you do anything that involves your man or his family, you'll need to ask him for permission first. This is one of the hardest things for a woman to do. *"Ok, Let's burn Frank and cut his balls off, he's a misogynistic narcissist! Women are not inferior and are not to be subjugated!"* Here's more gasoline for your fire...

You also need to ask his permission if you can share your feelings and questions with him; and even more so if he's busy doing something. If you don't, you're interrupting him and are being disrespectful. Unsolicited sharing is also a violation. *Need more gas...?*

You'll also need to ask him if he wants a massage, a blow job, or if you can make him a sandwich afterward. In short, never do anything unless he asks you for it. If all you do is bitch and complain and you can't express your feelings and needs in a vulnerable way, he'll feel like you're his mother—*gross.*

If you don't yet understand how to get into your feminine radiance, *asking for a man's permission is the ultimate cheat code and surefire way to put you in an absolute feminine polarity.* It's the most non-masculine form of communication you can do that will *instantly polarize him into his masculinity.* If he cowers or begins to domineer you as a result ... *run!* He's not masculine, or relationship material. If reading this hits a nerve, you're *masculinized* and also not ready or able to surrender to your femininity. When a man is honoured, he will feel so respected that he'll serve you like his Queen. When he hears, *"May I, Can I?"* or any other vulnerable form of communication, he will light up like a Christmas tree.

**Warning, never use this to manipulate him because he will sense it, even if it's unconsciously.*

Can you tell me how being feminine and using vulnerable communication is inferior when it inspires a man to give you inexhaustible devotion? How is it subservient when he wants to make the best possible decisions for both of you? *I'd say it's a definite advantage, to say the least.* Would you rather things remain as they are and support feminism which is destroying and masculinizing you to the point of being a total turn-off to men? Is waging war on masculine men and women who love them truly worth it? Is it working? *Being feminine is being strong!*

## SUBMISSION IS FREEDOM NOT SLAVERY

*"Submit? Fuck you! I bow to no one, especially to any man."* Let me guess, you're still single, or with an emasculated man who you secretly despise and wish grew some balls? Are you the same woman who rejects men's leadership and provision but will bend over backwards for your boss (who's male) to get paid? *"I also don't follow anyone... ever!"* Really? Women are natural followers, if they don't follow in their relationship they'll follow something; celebrities, fashion trends, and so on. Women are receptacles and open vessels that are imprinted upon. They receive what is given.

There's a stigma around the word *submission* and that it means subjugation, or being tied up and whipped with a gag in your mouth. *Submit* is a triggering word; its meaning has been distorted. I used to dance around it or avoid saying it altogether. It was much easier to evade the backlash and appease the politically correct machine than confront it. I can soften the word *submit* and change it to *receive...* if you'd like?

Many polarity teachings are also distorted. Domineering behaviour has been camouflaged to appear as dominance. These twisted doctrines also teach a man must penetrate his woman while she passively submits. Polarity coaches assert this as an absolute. Although polarity is firm as it is in nature, *nothing is completely rigid.* It's more of a dance; *his devotion guides her— her grace inspires him.* A woman isn't totally passive, nor is her pussy. She needs to offer some resistance; she's not someone who'll automatically surrender to being penetrated like fingers inserted into a bowling ball. Women are active, they invite and draw in. They coax like a flower's fragrance does to the bee. *True submission is done through a woman's authority, it's her choice... always.*

Submission is not for him, it's for you; it's how you respect and honour yourself. This is how you communicate your self-worth. Not *expressing your needs, feelings and desires* is not only disrespectful to him, but also to you. *You're denying your soul from feeling and expressing all its emotions.* You're betraying and deceiving yourself; you're covering your radiance and beauty up with blame and judgment. Denying you even have feeling and refusing they even exist is a form of self-punishment, which causes deep pain and suffering. You're responsible for expressing your value, no one else is.

What is so dishonourable about being *cherished, protected and provided* for? You're not losing yourself or your freedom. You're being honoured when you submit to a man. What a gift that is. Yes, initially it may appear it only benefits him, but it's a gift for both of you. He gifts you his leadership and your gift in return, is graciously receiving it. *You receive his strength and protection, he receives your connection, trust, intimacy, emotional support, and intuition.* You don't give up anything except for the pressure and need to lead and control. You can *just be* in radiance and finally begin to enjoy your life.

There's a difference between *submission* and being a *servant.* Submitting means to *receive without resistance,* to respect his leadership and to *surrender your control.* Many women can't because they're afraid of their femininity; they've become masculine and believe *being vulnerable equals pain.* Submission doesn't mean respecting *every single guy,* especially without vetting them. You're not a tramp, they have to earn your respect before you can trust them. If a man doesn't cherish and protect your heart, you have the power and authority to walk away from him. If he's riding the train off the rails, you'd be stupid not to jump off. You're not to surrender to a toxic and disloyal guy, nor to anyone for that matter.

You *surrender to yourself* so you can fully submit to your man and his leadership. *Never surrender to him.* A masculine man provides you with true submission, giving you the power to call *full stop* the moment you feel unsafe. Unlike domineering men, those who'll make you feel like you're trapped and in danger.

Do you know a man also needs to *submit* to the will of the Universe? If he doesn't, his life becomes chaotic; *resisting karmic laws will crush him.* His purpose needs to be in alignment with the Divine will. He needs to be inspired by something greater than himself.

## DRAMA & BROKEN DISHES

Some guys will call women drama queens. Although some are, many are simply misunderstood. Behind every *bitch* there's a *sweet girl* who's been hurt one too many times; one who has had enough of being treated like shit. These women don't know any other way to respond, it's their last resort. Guys, *if a woman is not being understood, she won't let up until she is.* You may call this persistence *drama,* she calls it *astonishment and her frustration; "Why can't I get through to you him?"* If you tune out because you can't deal with this behaviour, I caution you... if you neglect her, she'll withdraw and will stop caring. You can't blame her when she decides to seek attention elsewhere.

A woman will go into judgment when she feels anxious, confused or unsafe. She'll set boundaries and try to control the situation. You'll need to get her out of her head and stop her from overthinking. Her emotions will hold her hostage, if you try speaking logically, it'll make it worse. Allow her to express her feelings without judgment; she needs to feel safe doing so. *Correct her behaviour but never her feelings.* Remember, she's afraid of being hurt and taken advantage of, especially if she lets go of her control. Be mindful and lead her out.

Guys, give her your full *presence and love, feel her, see her, hear her, accept her and understand her fully and absolutely.* Lead her out of the fear and chaos without getting caught in it. Ladies, stop providing solutions and express your feelings vulnerably without blame or expectation. When he knows how you feel, he'll do his best to make things right. He won't be perfect at first, be patient. Let him screw up, and if he breaks a plate loading or unloading the dishwater, so be it. Yes, you're probably much better at it and will want to do it for him, but don't. This is mothering energy and it's depolarizing. You'll make him feel like he's an incompetent child. Not all guys are clueless, if given the chance they'll eventually figure it out. When you start respecting your man, you'll be amazed at how quickly he shifts. It may not be immediate, but he'll start leading and coming up with solutions all on his own.

When he feels valued, he feels good and will get off the couch. He'll begin to step it up and become motivated; he'll take charge and become more responsible. Even if he hates doing a particular chore, he'll do it for you because he loves you; he wants to please you and make your life easier. He'll only *be motivated* when he's doing it from *his leadership*, not from yours. He'll do so through *his solutions*, which are a result of *your vulnerable communication*. It won't work any other way because that's not how he's wired.

So, if you want men to respond, soften into your feminine energy and be open to receive his leadership and direction. Let him penetrate you. Remember, he won't respond to your orders, your whining or complaining. He'll feel extorted if you go into victim mode, or if you try manipulating him in any way. *The deeper you can go into your heart the better you'll be able to communicate with him.* If you find yourself going into warrior mode, you can keep fighting, or you can drop deeper into your feminine and express yourself vulnerably. You can shut down, or walk away.

Expressing your feelings is your true superpower and best option. If you can't give up your control, you'll be forever quarrelling with men, or attracting emasculated ones who put up with it. You may like having the upper hand over a guy, but there goes your respect and attraction for him. When a man with an integrated masculine polarity truly *feels your pain and vulnerability, it will inspire him to devote himself to you; absolutely.*

Learning a new language takes time, and even longer as we get older. I believe masculine/feminine communication should be taught when we're young, while our minds are still porous, malleable and sponge-like. Undoing years of programming may seem daunting, but can be done. A plant may have dried out inflexible stems, but they can be cut to make way for new pliable growth.

If you're still single, you have the advantage—a fresh start. Sure, it's more challenging when you're coupled because you need to uproot stronger and established patterns. Building muscle strength doesn't happen overnight, you'll need to have perseverance and be consistent. Those weights won't lift themselves. If you both want it and are committed to improving your communication and understanding, *it will happen.*

# POSTSCRIPT

## THERE IS STILL HOPE

We are here to experience life in the way we *choose* to live it and with those whom we resonate with. Theoretically, there's no right or wrong. There are however, natural laws in place whether we agree with them or not. Gravity doesn't care about feelings or preferences. If you jump off a cliff and believe you're a bird, you'll still plunge forcefully to the ground regardless. The *law of polarity is also absolute*; nature is always seeking balance and adjusts itself accordingly. If depolarization is causing an imbalance in your personal life or relationships, consider applying what you've learned here.

For better or worse, Gini is now out of the bottle, and Al wants to put her back in. Women have risen, and I don't know if they can ever go back to before July 13, 1848. The time when Elizabeth Cady Stanton and her four women friends helped start the empowerment movement by passionately expressing their discontent over tea at an impromptu get-together. The challenge we face today is learning how to navigate through this new paradigm and making it work for both sides of the gender brigade. We're sitting on a powder keg—guys are the barrel and women are the gunpowder. What's the solution? Who changes first?

Ultimately, *we all want to love and be loved back in return*; this seems easier said than done. Our past has impacted us, and we're all suffering from something that's blocking us from experiencing this. Sadly, we have very few role models to emulate; there aren't many ideal relationships or marriages available. *We both need to heal our wounds,* re-polarize and become an example for others. Let us rise not only for ourselves but for the world.

We've been fighting an un-winnable power struggle for too long. We need to course correct—it starts with us. Polarity doesn't care about gender politics or correctness. It is an organic response felt in the body, it's not known through the intellect.

If you're familiar with my first book, I briefly wrote about Divine masculine and feminine embodiments. I've purposely avoided discussing them in depth here. We aren't ready to explore such states until we've healed and understand our own polarity first. Our level of understanding, past experiences and our need to survive are holding us back from realizing this.

Regrettably, the majority of men have underdeveloped egos and use the feminine for personal gain and gratuitous pleasure. Sadly, women are complying, which is keeping this illusion going. The more we evolve spiritually the better we're able to integrate and balance our masculine and feminine polarities; a different and more equitable dynamic begins to unfold.

Men govern the *physical* realm, they're the builders of the material world. Women are the rulers of the *spiritual,* they're the healers and psychics of the unseen. Women help bring the minds of men to their hearts, men help women bring reason to theirs. Together, they bridge these worlds and both become more powerful as a result. This is why men are attacked and forced into being feminine, and why women are taught and encouraged to be masculine. The *powers that be* don't want us to awaken to our true power—*enlightened people can never become slaves.* We have more work to do until we can accomplish this. Until that time comes, we've got to enjoy the journey of self-exploration in solitude and through relationships.

## ACCOUNTABILITY

Guys, women need more than *your awareness, they need your full presence.* Never play with her heart, or seduce her with empty promises. They need less talk and more action from you. They've heard it all before and have been let down too many times. Your intentions may be good, but can you live up to them? Will you break her heart and prove you're just another bullshitter and bail when the going gets tough? Women have had enough, they've become jaded and have stopped believing in false promises. They have been forced into being masculine; they have been left with no choice. They don't want to be fooled again or to be left destitute. Many are left as single mothers needing to provide and protect for themselves, and their children.

Ladies, you aren't without fault either. Guys are willing to give you the world at first, but over time they lose all their motivation. Yes, some guys are selfish and truly don't care, but the majority do. You have a part in why he pulls away—whether it's from disrespecting him, putting out too fast, or over-mothering. Mostly, it's because of your masculine behaviour.

*Men need to mature and grow some balls; women need to learn emotional responsibility and how to be accountable for their behaviour.*

Guys, be willing to lose it all if she isn't on board with your mission and purpose. Walk if she isn't open to receiving you. If your *masculine leadership* isn't enough to soften her, then do what's best for you. I'm not suggesting you don't put in any effort, quite the opposite. But if you're banging against a stone wall, it isn't worth the frustration. Ladies, if he doesn't care about your heart, don't continue trying to control or change him. If your grace isn't enough to inspire him... *leave.* We have to know who needs to step it up, and it's not always the other person's fault. There shouldn't be any force, theatrics or ultimatums; there's only flow... towards or away... nothing more.

Ladies, if you don't want to soften into your feminine essence, that's your God-given right and choice. However, staying masculine may keep you eternally single and in relationships with simps who you'll grow to resent. Or, you'll be attracting guys who you'll be in continual power struggles with. Eventually, you'll become frustrated if you aren't already and will convince yourself there aren't any good men left. There's a saying, *"Make him feel like a man and he'll make you feel like a woman. Treat him like a boy and he'll treat you like his mother"*.

Likewise, guys, if you don't want to step into your masculine power and if you believe being nice will attract the woman of your dreams, you may also remain solo and in incompatible relationships.

## UNREALISTIC DEMANDS

Some of us fail to realize happiness in relationships is cultural and circumstantial—it's all about perspective. For some, having enough money to live *is happiness.* So is having children and grandchildren, things money can't buy. Marriage *was about survival, it has evolved and is more about romance and spiritual expansion.* Maybe we're so unhappy because we want things that are not a part of what a relationship should or can offer. We expect to marry the whole village and demand *one person* to personify every villager. We want our best friend, lover, spiritual confidant, travel buddy, foodie partner, and so on. *You may be waiting forever.* What if instead, you decided on how you'll show up and become the person you wanted to be with? When you *check off all the boxes yourself,* you'll be less hung on needing someone else to do it.

*Expectation* creates *dependence,* which influences our behaviour and almost always leads to *disappointment.* You can't avoid letdowns, all relationships will bring them to some degree. It happens whether it's at the hands of a lover, parent, child, family, or friend. Even God can disappoint us when we feel our prayers aren't answered. Adjust your expectations and stop asking one person to give you everything. No one is perfect, yet, we expect them to be. You may be lucky and find them, as we all deserve that. We have to be realistic about the odds. Lower *your expectations, not your standards,* and bring more to the table. I understand everything you've been through has made you *cautious,* you're not a *naive* teenager anymore. Nonetheless, be open and available to those who aren't typically *your type.* You may be in for a wonderful surprise.

I'd like to share one final jest before I bid you farewell. Men say, "Give a woman an inch, she'll take a mile". Women refute, "We only ask for an inch, but we're given a mile". Will we ever be in agreement or learn to understand each other? Perhaps not, but maybe one day... yes.

## IN CONCLUSION

This isn't the last chapter, it's a new beginning. Alternatively, you can continue repeating the same old story and hope for a plot twist. Or, you can use the information and tools I've shared with you and begin transforming not only your romantic life but your personal one as well. I believe understanding and embodying polarity is an integral part of the spiritual work needed to awaken on the path to self-realization.

Whatever your reason for being single is, however society has shaped you, and who you have become as a result, isn't a permanent condition; *it can be changed.* Before you know it, you'll be writing the follow-up to this book, *Why I'm not single— I Have An Amazing Relationship.*

Best regards,
Frank Di Genova

# Thank You For Reading

I offer courses, workshops, energy healing and 1:1 coaching. To learn more, visit:

www.frankdigenova.com

www.polarizedrelationships.com

The Ultimate Journey Awakening To Spirit Podcast

Thank you in advance

If you've enjoyed this book, I invite you to write a review. You can share it with your partner, pass it to a friend or a family member who will benefit.

Thank You

www.ingramcontent.com/pod-product-compliance
Lightning Source LLC
Chambersburg PA
CBHW051441050726
47593CB00005B/1870